Collins

Work on your
Grammar
Upper Intermediate B2

Collins

Published by Collins
An imprint of HarperCollins Publishers
Westerhill Road
Bishopbriggs
Glasgow
G64 2QT

HarperCollinsPublishers
Macken House,
39/40 Mayor Street Upper,
Dublin 1, D01 C9W8
Ireland

First edition 2013

14

© HarperCollins Publishers 2013

ISBN 978-0-00-749963-2

Collins® is a registered trademark of HarperCollins Publishers Limited

collins.co.uk/elt

A catalogue record for this book is available from the British Library

Typeset in India by Aptara

Printed and Bound in the UK by Ashford Colour Press Ltd

Specialists in Assessment and e-Learning

The material in this book has been written by a team from Language Testing 123, a UK-based consultancy that specializes in English language assessment and materials. The units are by Helen Chilton and have been based on material from the Collins Corpus and the Collins COBUILD reference range.

www.languagetesting123.co

Contents

Introduction

Welcome to *Work on your Grammar – Upper Intermediate (B2)*.

Is this the right book for me?

This book, *Work On Your Grammar – Upper Intermediate (B2)*, helps students to learn and practise English grammar at CEF level B2. This book is suitable for you to use if you are at CEF level B2, or just below.

So, what is CEF level B2? Well, there are six Common European Framework levels. They go up from A1 for beginners, A2, B1, B2, C1 and finally C2.

If the description below sounds like you, then this is probably the right book for you. If not, choose *Work on your Grammar – Intermediate (B1)* (below this level) or *Work on your Grammar – Advanced (C1)* (above this level).

- I can understand the main points and ideas when I read texts on many subjects, especially when they are about my areas of knowledge and interest.
- I can have conversations with native speakers of English and other good speakers in a quite natural way.
- I'm aware that I make mistakes, but other people usually understand what I want to say or write.
- I think I know quite a lot of grammar, but I also believe that there is a lot more to learn.

What does this book contain?

This book contains 30 units to help you learn and practise important grammar for upper intermediate (B2) level.

Each unit explains the **grammar point** and then there is a series of **exercises** that give you useful practice in this particular area. The exercises are there to help you really understand the grammar point and how to use it correctly. There are different types of exercise. This helps you to see different aspects of the grammar, and it means you have a range of practice to do.

The **answers** to all the exercises are at the back of the book.

Remember! boxes highlight important information about the grammar points, so it is a good idea to read them and think about them.

I'm a student: how can I use this book?

You can use this book in different ways. It depends on your needs, and the time that you have.

- If you have a teacher, he or she may give you some advice about using the book.

- If you are working alone, you may decide to study the complete book from beginning to end, starting with unit 1 and working your way through to the end.

- You might find that it is better to choose which units you need to study first, which might not be the first units in the book. Take control of what you learn and choose the units you feel are the most important for you.

- You may also decide to use the book for reference when you are not sure about a particular grammar point.

- You can find what you want to learn about by looking in the **Contents** page.

- Please note that, if you do not understand something in one Unit, you may need to study a unit earlier in the book, which will give you more information.

Study tips

1 Read the aim and introduction to the unit carefully.

2 Read the explanation. Sometimes, there is a short text or dialogue; sometimes there are tables of information; sometimes there are examples with notes. These are to help you understand the most important information about this grammar point.

3 Don't read the explanation too quickly: spend time trying to understand it as well as you can. If you don't understand, read it again more slowly.

4 Do the exercises. Don't do them too quickly: think carefully about the answers. If you don't feel sure, look at the explanation again. Write your answers in pencil, or, even better, on a separate piece of paper. (This means that you can do the exercises again later.)

5 Check your answers to the exercises in the back of the book.

6 If you get every answer correct, congratulations! Don't worry if you make some mistakes. Studying your mistakes is an important part of learning.

7 Look carefully at each mistake: can you now see why the correct answer is what it is?

8 Read the explanation again to help you understand.

9 Finally, if the unit includes a **Remember!** box, then try really hard to remember what it says. It contains a special piece of information about the grammar point.

10 Always return: come back and do the unit's exercises again a few days later. This helps you to keep the information in your head for longer.

I want to improve my grammar

Good! Only using one book won't be enough to really make your grammar improve. The most important thing is you!

Of course, you need to have a notebook, paper or electronic. Try these six techniques for getting the best from it.

- *Make it real*: It's probably easier to remember examples than it is to remember rules. Often, it's better to try to learn the examples of the grammar, not the explanations themselves. For example, rather than memorizing 'You can use the present simple to talk about the future', you should learn 'My holiday starts on Monday'.

- *Make it personal*: When you're learning a new structure or function, try to write some examples about yourself or people or places you know. It's easier to remember sentences about your past than someone else's! For example, 'I'm studying art this year'.

- *Look out*: Everything you read or hear in English may contain some examples of the new grammar you're learning. Try to notice these examples. Also, try to write down some of these examples, so that you can learn them.

- *Everywhere you go*: Take your notebook with you. Use spare moments, such as when you're waiting for a friend to arrive. Read through your notes. Try to repeat things from memory. A few minutes here and there adds up to a useful learning system.

- *Take it further*: Don't just learn the examples in the book. Keep making your own examples, and learning those.

- *Don't stop*: It's really important to keep learning. If you don't keep practising, you won't remember for very long. Practise the new grammar today, tomorrow, the next day, a week later and a month later.

I'm a teacher: how can I use this book with my classes?

The contents have been very carefully selected by experts from Language Testing 123, using the Common European Framework for Reference, English Profile, the British Council Core Inventory, the Collins Corpus and material created for *Collins COBUILD English Grammar*, *Collins COBUILD Pocket English Grammar* and *Collins COBUILD English Usage*. As such, it represents a useful body of knowledge for students to acquire at this level. The language used is designed to be of effective general relevance and interest to any learner aged 14+.

The exercises use a range of types to engage with students and to usefully practise what they have learnt from the explanation pages on the left. There are enough exercises for each unit that it is not necessary for students to do all the exercises at one sitting. Rather, you may wish to return in later sessions to complete the remaining exercises.

The book will be a valuable self-study resource for students studying on their own. You can also integrate it into the teaching that you provide for your students.

The explanations and exercises, while designed for self-study, can be easily adapted by you to provide useful interactive work for your students in class.

You will probably use the units in the book to extend, back up or consolidate language work you are doing in class. This means you will probably make a careful choice about which unit to work on at a particular time.

You may also find that you recommend certain units to students who are experiencing particular difficulty with specific language areas. Alternatively, you may use various units in the book as an aid to revision.

Lesson plan

1 Read the aim and introduction to the unit carefully: is it what you want your students to focus on? Make sure the students understand it.

2 Go through the explanation with your students. You may read this aloud to them, or ask them to read it silently to themselves. With a confident class, you could ask them to read some of it aloud.

3 If there is a dialogue, you could ask students to perform it. If there is a text, you could extend it in some way that makes it particularly relevant to your students. Certainly, you should provide a pronunciation model of focus language.

4 Take time over the explanation page, and check students' understanding using concept-checking questions. The questions will vary according to content, but they may be based on checking the time in verb tenses. For example, with the sentence, 'She came on the train that got here yesterday', you could ask, 'When did she arrive?'. This might elicit the correct answer 'yesterday' and the incorrect answer 'tomorrow', and you would know if your students understood the meaning of the past simple verb. Or you could ask, 'Where is she now?' and correct answers would include 'here' while incorrect answers would include 'on the train'.

5 Perhaps do the first exercise together with the class. Don't do it too quickly: encourage students to think carefully about the answers. If they don't feel sure, look together at the explanation again.

6 Now get students to do the other exercises. They can work alone, or perhaps in pairs, discussing the answers. This will involve useful speaking practice and also more careful consideration of the information. Tell students to write their answers in pencil, or, even better, on a separate piece of paper. (This means that they can do the exercises again later.)

7 Check their answers to the exercises in the back of the book. Discuss the questions and problems they have.

8 If the unit includes a **Remember!** box, then tell students to try really hard to remember what it says. It contains a special piece of information about the grammar point.

9 Depending on your class and the time available, there are different ways you could extend the learning. If one of the exercises is in the form of an email, you could ask your students to write a reply to it. If the exercises are using spoken language, then you can ask students to practise these as bits of conversation. They can re-write the exercises with sentences that are about themselves and each other. Maybe pairs of students can write an exercise of their own together and these can be distributed around the class. Maybe they can write little stories or dialogues including the focus language and perform these to the class.

10 Discuss with the class what notes they should make about the language in the unit. Encourage them to make effective notes, perhaps demonstrating this on the board for them, and/or sharing different ideas from the class.

11 Always return: come back and repeat at least some of the unit's exercises again a few days later. This helps your students to keep the information in their heads for longer.

1

Compound nouns

Nouns made out of two different nouns

In this unit you learn to use compound nouns made of two words.

There's a fabulous **swimming pool** overlooking the sea.

Nouns made out of two nouns

A compound noun is a noun that is formed from two words. You can write them as two words, a hyphenated word, or as one word. You use compound nouns when a single noun is not enough to refer clearly to a person or thing.

> *We've booked a holiday villa with a fabulous **swimming pool** overlooking the sea.*
> *I can't wait to have a **lie-in** tomorrow! It's been such a busy week.*
> *She went to bed with a terrible **headache**.*

Sometimes you can write a compound noun with or without a hyphen, or with or without a space.

You can write **air conditioning** or **air-conditioning**.

You can write **postbox** or **post box**.

Check in your dictionary to find out how you write the compound noun you want to use.

Once you know what is being referred to, you can sometimes use just the second word of a two-word compound noun.

> *What time does the **pool** open?*

In most compound nouns, the second word is a noun. However, the first word can be a noun, an adjective, a verb or a particle.

> *Have you seen my **address book**? (noun + noun)*
> *Lucy's going to **high school** in September. (adjective + noun)*
> *What time's **breakfast** in the morning? (verb + noun)*
> *The **in-laws** are coming for dinner. (particle + noun)*

-ing forms in compounds

Some compound nouns are formed by a *noun + -ing*.

> ***web surfing, water-skiing, dress-making***

You can also form compound nouns with *-ing + noun* to describe the function of something.

> ***sleeping tablet, swimming pool, running shoes***

Plurals

The plural form of a compound noun is usually the plural form of the second word.

> ***post offices, washing machines, car parks***

However, some compound nouns have a plural first word too.

> ***clothes shop → clothes shops***
> ***sales assistant → sales assistants***
> ***goods vehicle → goods vehicles***

Phrasal verbs

Some compound nouns are related to phrasal verbs. You can write these with a hyphen or as one word, but not two.

> ***mix-up, breakdown, takeaway, make-up***

The meaning of a compound noun is sometimes different from the words it consists of. For example, someone's **mother tongue** is not their mother's tongue but their first language; and **hay fever** is not a high temperature but an allergy.

Exercise 1

Match the sentence halves, as shown.

1 Dinner will be served in the dining   **a** juice and a bowl of cereal.

2 We forgot to take the tin   **b** room from 6 till 8 p.m.

3 Breakfast is normally fruit   **c** sink was blocked.

4 I had to call a plumber as the kitchen   **d** opener on our camping trip.

5 Please turn left at the traffic   **e** lights and carry straight on to the next junction.

Exercise 2

Put the correct word in each gap, as shown.

| alarm | tourist | aid | mobile | note | card | fiction | travellers' |

Dad: Have you packed your first [1]_____*aid*_____ kit? I hope you won't need it, but better to be safe than sorry.

Olivia: Yes, Dad. It's on my list of 'essentials', along with credit [2]_____ and [3]_____ cheques.

Dad: Good. Promise me you won't carry lots of cash around with you. It's dangerous. How about your [4]_____ clock? Won't that be important to catch all those early flights?

Olivia: No, I'm going to use my [5]_____ phone instead.

Dad: I don't want to interfere, but you're not taking all those science [6]_____ books with you are you? They'll make your luggage so heavy.

Olivia: You're probably right. I'll just take my e-book reader and download things.

Exercise 3

Rearrange the letters to find compound nouns, as shown. Use the definitions to help you. Decide whether the compound nouns should be one word or two.

1 yrdrrhaie ___*hairdryer*___ (a machine used to dry hair)
2 derosiad _____ (alongside a route used by vehicles)
3 ppltao _____ (a portable computer)
4 thealh ublc _____ (a place where you can go to get exercise)
5 oiueehswf _____ (a woman who does not have a paid job, but looks after her home and family instead)
6 rcashaw _____ (a place to take your car when it's dirty)

Exercise 4

Are the highlighted words correct or incorrect in the sentences?

1 Please get out your **science textbooks** ☑ and turn to page 20.
2 The event was so huge it required a team of **projects managers** ☐.
3 The café is closed but you can get some refreshments from the **drink dispenser** ☐ downstairs.
4 The cat was curled up on the **arm chair** ☐ in front of the fire.
5 Please buy a ticket at the **parkingmeter** ☐ and display it in your car window.
6 The Spice Girls were one of the most famous **girl bands** ☐ in the world.

Exercise 5

Are the highlighted words in this text formed correctly or incorrectly?

Receptionist: Hello. Can I help you?

Customer 1: Yes, I hope so. I've lost one of my ¹**ear rings** ☒ and I wonder if it's been handed in.

Receptionist: One moment please, I'll just have a look. Is this it?

Customer 1: Yes! Thanks so much. That's made my day.

Receptionist: No problem madam. And what can I do for you, sir?

Customer 2: I'm afraid I've lost my ²**sunglasses** ☐. They're quite expensive ones. I don't suppose anyone found them?

Receptionist: I'm terribly sorry but we haven't got them here. I'll look out for them though, OK? Ah, are you the lady who rang about the ³**creditcard** ☐?

Customer 3: That's right. If you remember, I've lost my whole ⁴**hand bag** ☐. It's got my ⁵**cheque book** ☐ and ⁶**memorystick** ☐ inside it too.

Receptionist: Well, not to worry, because I think we've got it.

Customer 3: Oh, thank goodness for that!

Exercise 6

Write the plural form of the compound noun in brackets to complete each sentence, as shown.

1 I'd like an appointment with one of your ____*lady doctors*____ (lady doctor) if possible.

2 There are more _____ (woman teacher) here than in most local schools.

3 Take That are one of the most successful _____ (boy band) since The Beatles.

4 If you need any help, please don't hesitate to ask one of our fully trained _____ (sales assistant).

5 Biology, chemistry and physics are all examples of _____ (science degree).

6 _____ (Heavy goods vehicle) should not attempt to drive over this bridge.

Exercise 7

Choose the correct word or words, as shown.

1 Shall we have a game of **table tennis** / **tabletennis** before lunch?

2 I took a course in **dresses making / dressmaking** so that I could start up my own tailoring business.

3 If you can't get any rest on long flights, it's a good idea to take a **sleep / sleeping** tablet.

4 For this job, you need a good working **knowledge / idea** of the relevant software.

5 Lesley works as a **career / careers** adviser for older teenagers.

6 You can use the **washing / wash** machine for your laundry.

Exercise 8

Complete the sentences by writing one word in each gap, as shown.

1 *Sunbathing* is less popular nowadays because people know that sunburn can be dangerous.

2 The film was a box _____ success but the critics hated it.

3 As a commuter, I find having a _____ ticket saves me several hundred pounds a year.

4 Please get into the car, put your hands on the _____ wheel and tell me whether the seat is in the correct position.

5 Spanish is my mother _____ but I also speak Portuguese fluently.

6 Film _____ get very little privacy; they're followed wherever they go.

Exercise 9

Match the two parts.

1 fitness   a assistant

2 goods   b stick

3 memory   c vehicle

4 sales   d shop

5 clothes   e centre

2

Countable and uncountable nouns

In this unit you learn to use countable and uncountable nouns in different ways.

Countable and uncountable nouns with different meanings

Some nouns can be countable or uncountable depending on their meanings.

exercise/exercises

*I don't do as much **exercise** as I should. (= physical activity)*
*Please complete **exercises** one to five for homework. (= practice of a subject)*

room/rooms

*My flat is so small, there's no **room** for my piano. (= not enough space)*
*How many **rooms** would you like to book? (= rooms in a house/hotel)*

light/lights

*Don't forget to switch the **lights** off when you leave the office. (= the lamps)*
*The **light's** perfect for taking photos today. (= the brightness of the day)*

Individual and mass nouns

Other nouns can be countable or uncountable depending whether you are thinking of them as individual items or are referring to things that together are a mass.

cake/cakes

*Have some **cake** – I made it this morning. (= a small piece of a large cake)*
*Those **cakes** look delicious! Let's get some for the party. (= individual cakes)*

hair/hairs

*Your **hair** looks lovely – have you had it cut? (= all the hair on someone's head)*
*Ugh! I've just found two **hairs** in my soup! (= individual hairs)*

fruit/fruits

*I don't eat much **fruit**. (= all fruit)*
*Shelly's been trying to grow tropical **fruits** on her terrace. (= a particular type of fruit)*

Zero article for generalizing with plural or uncountable nouns

When you use plural or uncountable nouns to talk about something **in general**, you don't use articles (**a**, **an** or **the**).

Coffee is too strong a flavour for many people. (NOT the coffee)
Paper is made from trees. (NOT the paper)
All anybody wants is to find true love. (NOT the true love)

Generalizing with singular countable nouns

When you want to talk in general about singular countable nouns, you use the definite article (**the**).

The desert is an inhospitable environment.
The elephant is one of the world's best-loved animals.
The wheel is man's most important invention.

Uncountable nouns with the definite article

When you want to refer to something specific, you use the definite article (**the**) with uncountable nouns.

The research carried out in this lab is ground-breaking. (= the research in this lab, not research in general)
The pollution in this area is the worst in the country. (= the pollution in this area, not pollution in general)
The work she does is highly specialized. (= the work she does, not work in general)

The definite article + musical instruments

When you talk about musical instruments, you always use **the**.

I'd love to learn to play the guitar.
Wow! You play the violin really well.

You also use **the** when talking about radio:

Do you listen to the radio much?

Exercise 1

Choose the correct word or words.

1 That story about the train robber has made the front page of all **papers / the papers** today.

2 Did you know that some **fruits / fruit** have lots more vitamins in them than others?

3 Please complete **the exercises / exercises** 1 to 10 in your workbooks for homework.

4 We can't get a bigger sofa because we don't have **a room / room** in this little flat.

5 Can you close the curtain please? The **light / lights** means I can't see the television clearly.

6 Do come and tell us all your adventures when you get home from your **travels / travel**.

Exercise 2

Put the correct word in each gap.

| music | coffee | cheeses | place | room | chocolates | apple |
| noise | exercise |

Sam: Right, let's make a shopping list. We've run out of [1]_____ but we've got other things to drink – there's tea and juices.

Jean: Yes, so what else? Should we get a box of [2]_____ to have something sweet after dinner tomorrow, when our friends are all coming?

Sam: Good idea. Where are they going to sit, by the way? There's not really enough [3]_____ around our little table.

Jean: No, I suppose some of us will have to sit in the lounge. We're going to have to be careful not to make a lot of [4]_____ this time. You must remember to keep the [5]_____ turned down! Otherwise the neighbours will complain again.

Sam: OK, yes. Right, back to the list. Let's get nice bread and a selection of [6]_____ to go with it.

Jean: Yes. Well, it's not a big list so shall we walk to the shop? I could do with some [7]_____.

Exercise 3

Find the wrong or extra word in each sentence, as shown.

1 ~~An~~ ice forms when water is at or below freezing point.
2 Origami is the craft of folding a paper to make models of animals, people and objects.
3 As e-book readers become increasingly popular, they are having a growing impact on the bookshops up and down the country.
4 Rents in this town are very high because so many students are looking for an accommodation while they are at university.
5 The far greater effort is required if we are to get rid of poverty.
6 A few years ago, cats overtook the dogs as the most popular domestic animal in the UK.

Exercise 4

Which sentences are correct?

1 How disgusting! I've just found two hairs in my soup! ❏
2 I've told you loads of time, don't borrow my things without asking. ❏
3 I was given a copy of Shakespeare's complete work but I doubt whether I'll read it. ❏
4 The research for this essay took Tim over six months. ❏
5 Not caring about eating is one sign of being in the love. ❏
6 Two coffee and one tea, please. ❏

Exercise 5

Write the singular or plural of the noun in brackets to complete each sentence, as shown. Add the definite article where necessary.

1 I'd like to learn to play ____*the guitar*____ (guitar) but I don't know a good teacher.

2 Are you still looking for _____ (work)? I've seen a job advert which you might be interested in.

3 I've lost my briefcase and it's got very important _____ (paper) in it.

4 After our swim, Dad bought _____ (ice-cream) for us from the van near the beach.

5 _____ (noise) of the rain on the window kept us awake.

6 I could see _____ (milk) all over the floor but there was no sign of the cat.

Exercise 6

Are the highlighted words correct or incorrect in the sentences?

1 **The** ❑ pollution in this town is terrible. I'm worried about our health.

2 New research suggests that **the** ❑ chocolate is good for you if eaten in small quantities.

3 Why bother to enrol at the gym to do **the** ❑ exercise? Why not just go for a jog instead?

4 **The** ❑ pandas are increasingly rare in the wild but there are quite a few in zoos around the world.

5 France is famous for **the** ❑ cheese. There are lots of different types.

6 For me, a holiday means being near **the** ❑ sea.

Exercise 7

Decide if the pairs of sentences have the same meaning, as shown.

1 A The computer has changed our lives.
  B This computer has changed our lives. ☒

2 A There aren't enough rooms in the hotel for all those people.
  B There isn't enough room in the hotel restaurant for all those people. ❑

3 A The blue whale is the largest mammal on earth.
  B Blue whales are the largest mammals on earth. ❑

4 A How many times did you ring Andy this morning?
  B How much time did you spend talking to Andy this morning? ❑

5 A Cats are popular pets in this country.
  B Lots of people in this country have a pet cat. ❑

Exercise 8

Match the sentence halves.

1	The chocolates	a	is made from cocoa, sugar and milk.
2	Chocolate	b	hair short.
3	As I swim a lot, I prefer to keep my	c	short dark hairs.
4	The baby was born with just a few	d	in that box taste absolutely delicious.
5	Everyone knows	e	exercises at home.
6	I think you should do your grammar	f	exercise is good for you.

Exercise 9

Choose the correct word or words.

[1]**The times / Times** have definitely changed since [2]**the computer / computer** was invented in the twentieth century.

No longer do we need to spend hours in the library doing [3]**the research / research**.

Instead, it's all there on our screen at home. It has also meant that [4]**travel / the travels** can be organized easily.

We can now book our flights and hotel online.

Inevitably, this means that some [5]**businesses / business** have closed, but on the other hand it creates [6]**work / works** in other industries.

Exercise 10

For each sentence, tick the correct ending.

1 Her parents are musicians, and she started playing
   ❏ violin when she was only 3 years old.
   ❏ the violin when she was only 3 years old.

2 I went to all the shops, but I couldn't find
   ❏ the coffee that she usually likes to drink.
   ❏ coffee that she usually likes to drink.

3 Although environmental groups are working hard to increase protected habitat,
   ❏ panda is still an endangered species.
   ❏ the panda is still an endangered species.

4 David tries not to eat too many cakes and biscuits because
   ❏ the sugar is very fattening.
   ❏ sugar is very fattening.

5 It was Alexander Graham Bell who
   ❏ invented telephone.
   ❏ invented the telephone.

6 I'm going to order a load of logs because
   ❏ wood is cheaper than coal at the moment.
   ❏ the wood is cheaper than coal at the moment.

3

Adjectives as nouns

In this unit you learn to use adjectives as nouns.

Hi Tim

We're currently on holiday in France. As you know, we love the **French** – their way of life, and their food! It's all very **enjoyable**, and we've saved the most enjoyable until last. We're going to stay in a luxury five-star hotel! Mark keeps saying the **most** expensive isn't necessarily the **best** and that hotel breaks are only for the rich, but I think if we both have a nice, relaxing time there, then some **good** will come of it.

See you soon!

Sarah

Tim Brown

101 High Street

Croydon

SW6 2JB

Using adjectives as nouns

You can use adjectives as nouns when you want to talk about groups of people who share the same characteristic or quality, for example, **the wealthy** and **the elderly**.

When you talk about these groups, you can use **the** + *adjective*, for example, **the rich** instead of *rich people*.

You never add **-s** to these adjectives even though there is more than one person in the group.

*The **poor** are disadvantaged in life. (NOT The ~~poors~~ are disadvantaged in life.)*

When the adjective being used as a noun is the subject of a verb you use a plural form of the verb:

*The young **don't** respect the elderly enough.*

If you want to talk about a more specific group of people, you put an adverb or another adjective in front of the verb:

*the **highly** educated, the **very** sick*

If you want to talk about two groups, you sometimes omit **the**. For example:

*There is an ever greater divide between **rich and poor**.*

With some words you can refer to how many people by putting a number in front of the adjective:

*There were **three injured** people.*

Nationality adjectives that end in **-ch**, **-sh**, **-se** or **-ss** can be used as nouns:

the French
the British
the Chinese
the Swiss

You use ordinal numbers and superlative adjectives as nouns:

the first
the third
the last
the best
the longest
the most expensive

> *Remember!*
>
> When you want to refer to the quality of something rather than to the thing itself, you can use the appropriate adjective. Sometimes it is used with **the** and sometimes without **the**. You will need to learn these uses.
> *Don't try and achieve **the impossible**. You'll only be disappointed.*
> *There's some **good** in all of us.*

Exercise 1

Match the sentence halves.

1 The rich   a is increasing as businesses close down.

2 The unemployed population   b are treated for their illnesses in this hospital.

3 The poor   c can get away with wearing outrageous clothes.

4 The elderly   d have recently had an increase in their pensions.

5 Only the young   e can afford to buy anything they want.

6 All the sick in the area   f often find it difficult to manage on their wages.

Exercise 2

Complete the sentences by writing one word in each gap.

| farthest | worst | fourth | most | tallest | first |

1 Joanna was early as usual – she was the _____ to arrive at the party.

2 All of the maths results were bad, but Jake's were the _____.

3 The _____ expensive isn't always the best.

4 Sophie was disappointed to only come _____ in the race.

5 Our apartment block is the _____ in the city.

6 Let's have a competition to see who can run the _____.

Exercise 3

Put each sentence into the correct order, as shown.

1 best / the / only / enough / good / is / my / boss / for / .
   Only the best is good enough for my boss.

2 have / always / the / good / French / produced / wine / .
   _____

3 were / last / we / the / to / arrive / .
   _____

4 isn't / always / the best / the biggest / for / value / money / .
   _____

5 holiday / on / went / Ted / the / week / last / before / .
   _____

6 second / his / album / great / is / .
   _____

Exercise 4

Complete the sentences by writing one word in each gap.

| sick | best | rich | good | unemployed | British |

1 The _____ need help if they are going to find work during a recession.

2 There is some _____ in all of us.

3 Doctors and nurses look after the _____.

4 Robin Hood was a legendary English outlaw who stole from the _____ and gave to the poor.

5 The _____ hold elections every five years.

6 The _____ is yet to come – you just have to be patient.

Exercise 5

Which sentences are correct?

1 You can always rely on a French to produce excellent food. ❏

2 This is the closest we've come to success. ❏

3 Charities do a lot of the good for people in need. ❏

4 Jack is always the first to admit when he's wrong. ❏

5 A rich can afford to buy lots of expensive things. ❏

6 The cheapest isn't always the worst quality. ❏

Adjectives + to-infinitive

Using adjectives with linking verbs to talk about people and things

In this unit you learn to use adjectives with the **to**-*infinitive* clause.

| To: John McMullan |
| From: Matthew Beattie |
| Subject: Universities |

Hi John!

How are you?

I'm sitting at my desk but I'm not working – it's **far too** hot to work, and what I'm doing isn't interesting **enough** for me to concentrate on!

Anyway, I need help. Would you be willing **to** give me some advice? I'm thinking about which university to go to, and some of them are just too far away **for** me to consider.

But apart from that I'm quite **easy** to please, so it shouldn't be too difficult for **you** suggest somewhere you think would be good to study....

Hope to hear from you soon.

Matthew

Using adjectives with verbs to talk about people and things

After a linking verb like **be** you often use an adjective + **to**-*infinitive* to describe how someone feels about a situation or action.

*She **was pleased to see** me.*
*I **was relieved to pass** my exams.*

You often use a **to**-*infinitive* clause to talk about the future.

*Would you **be happy to pick me up** after the concert?*
*She **was keen to get** home early.*

Some adjectives aren't usually used alone and have a **to**-*infinitive* clause after them to show what situation or action the adjective relates to.

*We're **bound to be** late for school.*
*I'm **willing to try** anything once.*

When you want to express an opinion about someone or something, you use an adjective + the **to**-*infinitive*.

> *This work is **impossible to do**.*
> *Was I **wrong to blame** her for the accident?*

You can also use adjectives with **to**-*infinitive* after **it**.

> ***It** was good of Michael **to help** me paint the house.*
> ***It's** easy **to make** children laugh.*

Giving opinions

(*not*) adjective + *enough* + (*for* X) *to* + infinitive

You can use **enough** after an adjective with the **to**-*infinitive* to give an opinion.

> *That looks **good enough to eat**!*
> *Trains aren't **punctual enough** for us **to rely on** round here.*

(*much, far*) *too* + adjective + (*for* X) *to* + infinitive

You can also use **too** before an adjective with the **to**-*infinitive* to give an opinion.

> *Oh, that curry's **far too hot to eat**.*
> *It's **much too naughty to eat** chocolate!*

Exercise 1

Match the sentence halves.

1 My sister is difficult		**a**	to find – it was clearly signposted.
2 Are you willing		**b**	to discover her work hadn't been saved on the computer.
3 The library wasn't hard		**c**	to find out who had called him.
4 Ben was curious		**d**	to please – it's always hard to buy presents for her.
5 I was amazed		**e**	to work late? We've got a big order to fill.
6 Sarah was concerned		**f**	to hear I'd won the competition!

Exercise 2

Complete the sentences by writing one word in each gap.

wasn't	too	for	enough	far	weren't

1 The dress was _____ too expensive for Sarah to buy.

2 That car isn't reliable _____ to use regularly.

3 The hotel was _____ far away for us to walk to.

4 I _____ quick enough to catch the glass when it fell.

5 The sea wasn't warm enough _____ us to go swimming.

6 The sandwiches in the café _____ fresh enough, so we went somewhere else.

Exercise 3

Choose the correct word.

1 This coffee is much too **full / hot / small** for me to drink straight away.

2 It's far too **wet / sunny / freezing** to work outside today – we'll get soaked.

3 This cake looks almost too **easy / fresh / good** to eat – I can't wait to try some!

4 This drink isn't really **suitable / healthy / correct** enough for children to drink.

5 I don't think Jamie is **old / small / shy** enough to go out on his own yet.

6 It's much too far for us to **walk / drive / travel**, so we'll have to go in the car.

Exercise 4

Write the missing words in sentence B so that it means the same as sentence A.

1 A The water was too cold for us to go swimming.

  B The water wasn't warm _____ for us to go swimming.

2 A Is it OK if you work late tonight?

  B Are you happy _____ late tonight?

3 A We didn't find it difficult to climb to the top of the hill.

  B It was easy _____ to climb to the top of the hill.

4 A This drink has got lots of sugar in it – I can't drink it!

  B This drink is _____ too sweet for me to drink.

5 A The windows on the bus were too dirty to see through.

  B The windows on the bus _____ clean enough to see through.

6 A Jack discovered to his astonishment that he'd won a prize!

  B Jack was _____ discover that he'd won a prize!

Exercise 5

Put each sentence into the correct order.

1 very / isn't / David / to / difficult / persuade / .

_____

2 not / easy / to / it's / find / restaurants / good / .

_____

3 too / for / it's / me / work / hot / to / .

_____

4 tea / isn't / enough / the / for / hot / Max / drink / to / .

_____

5 was / see / Pat / to / his / amazed / TV / friend / on / .

_____

6 dress / far / the / too / was / for / small / Sally / wear / to / .

_____

5

Using adjectives in phrases to talk about people and things

In this unit you learn to use gradable and ungradable adjectives. You also learn about opposites and compounds of adjectives.

Using adjectives in phrases to talk about people and things

There are two main types of adjective: qualifying adjectives and classifying adjectives. Qualitative adjectives describe the qualities that someone or something has, and classifying adjectives show the class that something belongs to.

Gradable adjectives

Qualitative adjectives describe a quality that someone or something has, for example, **pretty**, **funny**, **interesting**, **difficult**.

> I like Fern – she's a **lively** girl.
> I'm reading an **interesting** book at the moment.

Qualitative adjectives are gradable. This means you can use them with adverbs like **very**, **fairly**, **rather** and **slightly**.

> This coffee's **very** bitter. I can't drink it.
> I'm **rather** tired of all this noise! Please be quiet.

You can also make comparative and superlative forms of qualitative adjectives, for example, **taller**, **the cheapest**, **the most intelligent**.

> Stephanie's **much taller than** Anthony.
> Pepe is **the most intelligent** person in our class.

Ungradable adjectives

Classifying adjectives tell us the class that something belongs to.

> They need **financial** help. (= the kind of help they need)
> The country has a lot of **social** problems. (= the kind of problems the country has)

Classifying adjectives are ungradable. This means you can use them with adverbs like **totally**, **completely** and **absolutely**.

> It was **completely unnecessary** to close the factory down.
> The children are being **totally impossible** today!

Classifying adjectives do not have comparative or superlative forms.

> ### Remember!
>
> You can't use adverbs like **totally**, **completely** or **absolutely** with gradable adjectives (*He's totally nice. It's absolutely difficult*) and you can't use adverbs like **very**, **fairly** or **slightly** with classifying adjectives (*The situation is very terrible. This puzzle is slightly impossible*).
>
> You can use **really** with both gradable and ungradable adjectives (*I'm really happy at the moment. The weather's really terrible.*)

Forming adjective opposites

You can make the opposite of an adjective by adding a prefix, such as **un-** or **in-**, for example, **un**happy, **dis**agreeable, **im**possible, **ir**responsible.

There is no rule about which prefix to use. Use your dictionary to check the opposite of the adjective you want to use.

Compound adjectives

You can make compound adjectives with two or more words. These compounds usually have a hyphen between the words. Compound adjectives can be qualitative, classifying or colour adjectives.

*Today we went on a **ten-kilometre** walk.*
*He's a **good-looking** guy.*
*She wore a **sky-blue** dress.*

Exercise 1

Match the sentence halves.

1 The cake was absolutely	a nervous about her first day at work.
2 John's just got a new job, and he seems fairly	b unsuitable for children – it's too difficult.
3 Is it completely	c slow in this restaurant.
4 Simone's sister felt slightly	d ruined as it was in the oven too long.
5 I must admit, the service is rather	e necessary to fill in lots of forms?
6 This game is totally	f happy with how it's going.

Exercise 2

Choose the correct word.

1 That was **an absolutely / a slightly / a fairly** terrible film!

2 He's **a completely / an absolutely / a rather** strange man.

3 Jake was **completely / very / slightly** exhausted when he got home.

4 It's **rather / extremely / absolutely** freezing in here when the heating's not working.

5 Sam was **extremely / totally / perfectly** disappointed to hear the news.

6 Sandra thought the theatre play was **completely / quite / totally** good.

Exercise 3

Put the adjectives in the gaps to show how they make opposites, as shown.

> legal | responsible | possible | satisfied | believable | satisfied
> important | convenient

1 un + _believable_ _important_ _satisfied_

2 im + _____

3 dis + _____

4 il + _____

5 in + _____

6 ir + _____

Exercise 4

Choose the correct word.

1 My dad often goes for a three- **part / mile / step** walk before breakfast.

2 The film had such a fast-**running / going / moving** story that I could hardly follow what was happening.

3 My uncle is a **kind / deep / caring**-hearted man who always wants to help everyone.

4 Jake is a **fair / mean / good**-looking young man, as well as being clever.

5 My boss expected me to read a 30-**page / line / word** document in the five minutes before the meeting, which was impossible, of course.

6 The dress was so **bad / old / poor**-fashioned that I couldn't possibly wear it.

Exercise 5

Write the missing words in sentence B so that it means the same as sentence A, as shown.

1 A Everyone agreed that Jake hadn't behaved responsibly.
  B Jake's behaviour was seen as _irresponsible_.

2 A The beach was two hours from the village by bus.
  B There was a _____ bus journey to the beach from the village.

3 A It's five degrees colder than it was yesterday
  B There's been a _____ drop in temperature.

4 A We were late because we got stuck behind a vehicle that was moving very slowly.
  B Our late arrival was due to a _____ vehicle in front of us.

5 A My house is two minutes away from here on foot.
  B It's a _____ walk from here to where I live.

6 A The criminal showed no understanding of what we mean by morals.
  B The criminal seemed to be completely _____.

Participle clauses

Clauses at the beginning of sentences to give information about the situation

-ing and -ed forms

In this unit you learn to make participle clauses in the present and past using **-ing** and **-ed** forms.

Being a fashion designer,
she always wears fabulous clothes.

Clauses at the beginning of sentences

You give more information about a situation by adding a clause beginning with an **-ing** participle or an **-ed** participle.

> *Being a fashion designer, she always wears fabulous clothes.*
> *Exhausted by all the work I'd done, I went to bed early.*

You use participle clauses to express a condition, reason, cause, result or time. They are useful in writing because we can say the same thing but with fewer words. Compare:

> *Realizing she'd said the wrong thing, she apologised immediately.*
> *When she realized that she had said the wrong thing, she apologised immediately.*

-ing clauses

You use the **-ing** participle to talk about both present and past events.

> *Being shorter than average I can never reach the top shelf!*
> *Having confessed his mistake, he begged for forgiveness.*

Participle clauses with conjunctions and prepositions

You can use participle clauses after conjunctions and prepositions, for example, **when**, **while**, **before**, **after**, **on**, **without**, **instead of**. This is usually with the *-ing* clause.

*I broke my leg **while skiing** in the mountains.*
*Please take a shower **before entering** the pool.*

Negative participle clauses

You can also make negative participle clauses by putting **not** before the *-ing* or *-ed* form.

***Not feeling well**, I decided to leave early.*
***Not having finished** the project, I had to work late.*

having been + past participle

You can use the passive structure **having been** + *past participle*.

***Having been told off** for arriving late, I knew I couldn't do it again.*

This structure is also an alternative to a clause with **since**.

***Having been out of the country** for a few years, I found it difficult to get used to being home. (= Since I had been out of the country for a few years, I found it difficult to get used to being home.)*

Remember!

You don't use participle clauses much in speech as they are too formal.
Instead of:
Seeing the traffic jam ahead, I turned my car round and went back home
You would say:
***I saw** the traffic jam ahead, so I turned my car round and went back home.*

Dangling participles

Look at this example:

Walking through the woods, the birds chirped loudly.

Logically, it sounds like the birds are walking through the woods. This is because the subject of the main clause (the birds), are assumed to be the subject of the phrase attached to the main clause (Walking through the woods ...). The real subject is a person.

It's better not to use dangling participles in writing. You can say instead:

As I was walking through the woods, the birds chirped loudly.

Exercise 1

Which sentences are correct?

1 Hurrying to catch the train, it arrived just as I reached the station. ❑

2 Being rather afraid of having nightmares, Paul didn't want to watch a horror film. ❑

3 I decided to go home, disappointed by the poor performance. ❑

4 Having been paid to perform for just an hour, the band actually played for twice as long. ❑

5 Disagreed about the fastest route to take, Ian and Sylvia ended up spending far too long on the journey. ❑

6 The film was surprisingly good, having already seen it once. ❑

Exercise 2

Are the highlighted words correct or incorrect in the sentences?

1 **Being** ❑ somewhat hard of hearing, everyone had to speak quite loudly so that the man knew what was going on.

2 I was able to lead the way directly to the restaurant, **having** ❑ been there several times before.

3 Not **being qualified** ❑ , Simon found it difficult to get a job as an accountant.

4 **Rejecting** ❑ by the voters, the former Member of Parliament decided to withdraw from politics.

5 **Protected** ❑ from the intense cold by her warm clothes, the woman set out into the snow.

6 The TV series was cancelled halfway through its run, **not having achieved** ❑ the popularity that was expected.

Exercise 3

Decide if the pairs of sentences have the same meaning.

1 **A** On hearing the news of Will's engagement, Sally realized she was still in love with him.
   B When Sally heard the news of Will's engagement, she realized she was still in love with him. ❑

2 **A** Battered by a hurricane, the town was largely rebuilt.
   B When the town had been largely rebuilt, it was battered by a hurricane. ❑

3 **A** Not having studied any foreign languages at school, Trevor realized a job involving international travel wouldn't be suitable for him.
   B Trevor realized a job involving international travel wouldn't be suitable for him because he hadn't studied any foreign languages at school. ❑

4 **A** Having lost the necklace Jack had given her, Miriam decided to buy a new one.
   B Miriam decided to buy a new necklace, in case she lost the one Jack had given her. ❑

5 **A** Situated in a beautiful wooded valley, the village is a popular tourist destination.
   B The village, which is a popular tourist destination, is situated in a beautiful wooded valley. ❑

Exercise 4

Complete the sentences by writing one word or phrase in each gap.

| Having shared | Being learnt | Learnt | Being shared | Separating |
| Learning | Separated | Having learnt | | |

1 _____ at birth, the twins had led amazingly similar lives.

2 _____ some years ago what to do in a medical emergency, I feel confident I can deal with any problems that arise.

3 _____ by heart, poems can provide pleasure and consolation in any situation.

4 _____ a flat with three other students when he was at university, Matthew found it hard to live alone.

5 _____ the victim from his attacker, Francis realized who he had helped.

6 _____ from everything that goes wrong, I'm resolved to be more cautious in future.

Exercise 5

Write the missing words in sentence B so that it means the same as sentence A.

1 **A** Leslie would make a good travelling companion because he has a good sense of humour.

   B _____ a good sense of humour, Leslie would make a good travelling companion.

2 **A** Magda had practised the violin for many years, so she was quite an accomplished player.

   B _____ the violin for many years, Magda was quite an accomplished player.

3 **A** Jean was injured in a riding accident when she was a child, so she is nervous around horses.

   B _____ in a riding accident when she was a child, Jean is nervous around horses.

4 **A** Polly has had to improve her map-reading skills, because she gets lost at frequent intervals.

   B _____ at frequent intervals, Polly has had to improve her map-reading skills.

Exercise 6

Choose the correct word or phrase to fill each gap.

1 **Stopped / Stopping** by the police, the driver had to explain why he had been using his mobile phone.

2 **Recognizing / Having been recognized** by a journalist, the actress couldn't deny who she was.

3 **Not having travelled / Not travelling** by plane before, the child was very excited.

4 **Taking / Taken** once a day, these pills will control your symptoms.

5 **Not being / Not having been** in touch for all these years, I must apologize for contacting you out of the blue.

6 **Having been allowed / Allowing** to go out on his own for the first time, Johnny felt very grown up.

7

Expressions to show the purpose of actions and people

in order to, so, so as to

In this unit you learn how to use certain expressions to show the purpose of actions and people.

Purpose

You use a purpose clause to say what someone's intention is when they do something. The most common type of purpose clause is with the **to**-*infinitive*.

> *Penguins huddle together **to keep warm**.*
> *People would stroll down the path **to admire the garden**.*
> *Farmers have put up barricades **to prevent people from moving onto their land**.*

A purpose clause needs a main clause to make a complete sentence. It usually comes after the main clause.

> *She changed her job **to have more free time**. (She changed her job = main clause)*

You can also use **in order to**, **so**, **so as to** and **so that** to show purpose.

> *We need to set off early **in order to** allow for the traffic being busy.*
> *Can I borrow your laptop **so** I can do my homework in my bedroom?*
> *I sleep with my window open **so as to** let in the fresh air.*

Some purpose clauses contain a modal verb. If the main clause is in the present, you use the modals **can**, **may**, **will** or **shall**.

> *I'll do my homework quickly **so I can** go for a bike ride with my friends.*
> *I've drawn a map **so you'll** find my house more easily.*

If the main clause is in the past, you use **could**, **might**, **should** or **would** in the purpose clause.

> *He said he'd pick me up early **so we could** have something to eat before the concert.*

You can also make purpose clauses negative by adding **not**.

> *They tiptoed up the stairs so as **not** to wake the children.*
> *I took plenty to read in order **not** to be bored on the plane.*

Result

You use **so** and **so that** in result clauses to talk about the result of an action or situation.

*She's worked really hard on her spelling, **so** she feels more confident about writing in English.*
*My suitcase had got lost **so that** I had to wear my sister's clothes all holiday.*

You can also use **so that** to say that something is or was done to achieve a particular result.

*Please speak more slowly **so that** I can understand you.*
*Dad unplugged the TV in my bedroom **so that** I couldn't watch it in bed.*

You can also use **so ... that** to talk about the result of an action or situation.

*He ran **so** quickly **that** I couldn't catch up with him.*
*She was **so** surprised **that** she dropped her coffee.*

Exercise 1

Match the sentence halves.

1 These regulations have been put in place

2 They took a later train

3 Ralph decided to start saving a certain amount each month

4 We need to set off in the next few minutes

5 You should start taking regular exercise

6 I'll have to start revising for my exams

a so as not to miss the plane.

b in order to make the booking process as fair as possible.

c so I stand a chance of passing.

d so as to benefit from the lower fares.

e to improve your health and fitness.

f in order to buy a new car.

Exercise 2

Complete the sentences by writing one word in each gap.

1 Jimmy slowed down in order _____ let the car behind overtake him.

2 The Council has modified its rules in _____ to make public participation easier.

3 Both parties must sign this contract so _____ to commit themselves to the project.

4 These recordings are available in a variety of formats so _____ everyone is able to find one they can play.

5 All litter should be taken home so as _____ to spoil the enjoyment of other visitors to the park.

6 The committee had spent six months planning the event, _____ it went without a hitch.

Exercise 3

Find the wrong or extra word in each sentence.

1 A party was arranged so to celebrate the team's success.

2 Jeremy walked as slowly as he could so as that he wouldn't reach home before his parents had gone out.

3 They built a brick wall round their garden in the order to prevent rabbits from getting in.

4 The book has been organized thematically so that as to highlight developments over a period of time.

5 More research needs to be carried out, in order to be confirm the validity of the findings.

6 Many people choose to go to university in order they to command a higher starting salary when they enter employment.

Exercise 4

Choose the correct phrase to fill each gap.

1 Louis moved carefully **so as not to / so that not / in order not** disturb the people sleeping around him.

2 We waited for the sky to clear **in order / so that / so as** we could take photographs of the stars.

3 Many universities have launched international advertising campaigns **in order to / so that / so as** boost the number of students from around the world.

4 It would be worth installing a wood-burning stove **so not to / not in order that / in order not to** freeze during the cold, hard winters.

5 The concert venue was changed **so that / in order to / in order** a larger audience could be accommodated.

Exercise 5

Which sentences are correct?

1 A bridge was constructed across the river so as to shorten the journey by road. ❏

2 A city bypass was planned so that reduce traffic in the centre. ❏

3 The viaduct was strengthened in order it would cope with the rapidly increasing traffic using it. ❏

4 The cinema was equipped with high-quality sound equipment so that it could present live music and drama transmitted from elsewhere. ❏

5 We need to go to the garden centre so we can look for some shrubs for the garden. ❏

6 The porcelain vase fell from the top shelf of the cupboard so that it broke. ❏

8

Expressions to show the connection between events and situations

while, since

In this unit you learn to make a concession, contrast two statements and give reasons for something.

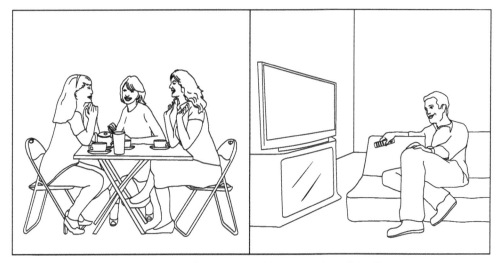

Jenny loves to go out with her friends, **while** her husband prefers to stay at home.

Concession

You can join two statements together with a concessive clause. To **concede** (noun **concession**) something means to admit or acknowledge that something is true or correct. When you want to do this, you join the two clauses together with **while**.

> *While you may be right about the cost, I still don't think we should change our plans.*
> *While Tony agreed that the interviewee was a nice person, he didn't offer her the job.*

Contrast

This allows you to make a contrast between the statements, or make one of them seem surprising. You can use different words to help you do this, for example, **while** or **whereas**.

> *While I'd like to go to the party, I'd also like to stay at home.*
> *Jenny loves to go out with her friends, **while** her husband prefers to stay at home.*

Whereas is more formal than **while**.

> *At this school boys do better in science subjects, **whereas** girls do better in the arts.*
> *The average woman in Britain is about 164cm tall, **whereas** the average man is about 177cm.*

You can sometimes use **while** in **-ing** participle clauses.

> ***While** he thinks horses are beautiful, he's also a little scared of them.*
> → ***While thinking** horses are beautiful, he's also a little scared of them.*

Reason

When you want to give the reason for something, you use a reason clause. You can use the words **since** and **as** to help you do this.

since

> *I had no idea that she was a doctor, **since** we'd never discussed our careers.*
> ***Since** you didn't tell me what time you were coming home, I haven't made you any dinner!*

as

> *We went to Helen's house after school, **as** she had some computer games we wanted to try.*
> ***As** it was a cold, sunny day, we wrapped up warm and went for a walk.*

Exercise 1

Decide if the pairs of sentences have the same meaning.

1 **A** The average mark for full-time students was 60%, whereas the average for part-timers was 50%.
   B The average mark for full-time students was 60%, while the average for part-timers was 50%. ❑

2 **A** Since you've had more experience with computers, could you download the software for me?
   B You've had a lot of experience with computers, so why did you download the software for me? ❑

3 **A** As we're running late, I'll summarize the rest of the points I have to make.
   B In case we're running late, I'll summarize the rest of the points I have to make. ❑

4 **A** I won't say any more now, as you obviously know more about the matter than I do.
   B I won't say any more now, since you obviously know more about the matter than I do. ❑

5 **A** I had only just begun my training session, whereas the rest of the team had been warming up for some time.
   B I had only just begun my training session, but the rest of the team had been warming up for some time. ❑

Exercise 2

Are the highlighted words correct or incorrect in the sentences?

1 The idea here is to find out whether the students are familiar with the basic chemical structures, **whereas** ❑ the next course will deal with more advanced material.

2 **As** ❑ there were no violins available, the studio manager suggested using guitars, which worked surprisingly well.

3 **Since** ❑ most shoppers may be quite happy to order online, there are some goods which still need to be examined before buying them.

4 My aim was to discover which means of transport was cheapest, **while** ❑ my employers wanted to know which was the least expensive.

5 I'll ask my teacher if we can have the afternoon off, **as** ❑ I don't think he'll agree to it.

6 Perhaps you could explain what this means, **since** ❑ you seem to know so much about the subject.

Exercise 3

Which sentences are correct?

1 I decided not to buy the jacket as it was just what I wanted. ❑

2 Laurie is very particular about his appearance, while Frankie spends hours getting ready to go out. ❑

3 Since I have little knowledge of the subject, I find it hard to give an opinion. ❑

4 The rooms downstairs are all clean and tidy, whereas upstairs everything is in excellent order. ❑

5 While I accept that some people don't enjoy competitive sport, I believe that everyone should try to take some form of exercise. ❑

6 As the train arrived very late, we had time to eat while we were waiting. ❑

Exercise 4

For each sentence, tick the correct ending.

1 I enjoy camping and hiking, whereas
   ❑ my brother does too.
   ❑ my brother likes the comfort of a hotel.

2 While rain is certainly a possibility,
   ❑ there's no need to cancel our walk.
   ❑ it's a good idea to take umbrellas.

3 You'd better phone for a taxi now,
   ❑ as one may not be able to come immediately.
   ❑ even one may not be able to come immediately.

4 Alice may have an American passport,
   ❑ since she was born in the States.
   ❑ though she was born in the States.

5 Air travel is fast but you have to spend a lot of time at the airport,
   ❑ also going by road is slower but you travel door to door.
   ❑ while going by road is slower but you travel door to door.

Exercise 5

Match the sentence halves.

1 I haven't brought a drink with me   a as I can get one at a café.

2 I don't often eat a big lunch,   b since we may not get anything to eat later.

3 Since I haven't had breakfast,   c whereas my father always does.

4 While you may not be thirsty,   d I need to have a snack some time soon.

5 I think we should have a sandwich,   e we all want a cold drink.

Exercise 6

Choose the correct word.

1 **Since / So / Even** all the other seats are full, we'll have to sit at the back.

2 I don't listen to music when I'm working, **but not / whereas / as** my husband has it on all the time.

3 **If / Because / While** the traffic may be bad, at least the roads are well-maintained.

4 I decided to buy some new boots **as / while / but** I'd just had a lot of money for my birthday.

5 My older brother is crazy about motorbikes **as / while / so** my younger one only cares about football.

Exercise 7

Decide if the pairs of sentences have the same meaning.

1 A While she may seem shy at parties, she speaks out quite confidently in class.
  B She is much more confident in class than she is at parties.

2 A While Ali wanted to resign in protest, he knew that he needed the money from the job.
  B Ali decided to leave his job because it didn't pay enough money.

3 A While I think Maria's a nice person, I don't want to make a friend of her.
  B I'm not sure if Maria is nice enough to be my friend.

4 A Giuseppe drinks coffee all day long, while Anna only ever drinks tea.
  B Giuseppe drinks coffee all day long, because Anna only ever drinks tea.

5 A Lots of people nowadays buy products and services online, whereas I still prefer to do my shopping in person.
  B I don't like to use a computer to do my shopping.

6 A While I don't want to offend her, I do think someone should tell her she's behaved badly.
  B I'm too scared of offending her to tell her that she's behaved badly.

9

Adverbs to show opinion about situations

In this unit you learn to use adverbs to make your opinion clear about a situation.

CONFERENCE REPORT
Annual Sales Conference, Harrogate, 9 May

The conference got off to a good start with an excellent speech by the president. **Disappointingly**, a number of people were held up by traffic and missed this. However, it is available online, **fortunately**.

There were plenty of discussion groups. **Generally**, these were well attended and found to be useful.

The attendance figures for the evening talks, however, were **undoubtedly** low compared to other years.

Inevitably, the fact that this year's conference was in a town with so many good restaurants was largely to blame for this!

In theory, there should be no similar problems next year, when we will be in a conference centre near a small village.

For details of all conference talks, please see the association website.

Adverbs to show opinion about situations

When you want to make your opinion clear, you can use a commenting adverbial. Here's a list of common adverbials which help you to show what your attitude is:

amazingly	personally
apparently	presumably
as far as I'm concerned	rightly
disappointingly	seriously
fortunately	stupidly
frankly	to my mind
funnily enough	to my surprise / astonishment
generally	typically
honestly / in all honesty	unbelievably
in my opinion / view	understandably
in theory	undoubtedly
obviously	unexpectedly
on reflection	wisely

These adverbials usually (but not always) go at the beginning or end of a sentence.

To be honest, I never really liked Amanda's boyfriend.
Oh, you've bought that book! I got it myself yesterday, funnily enough.

Sometimes you can also put the adverbials in the middle of the sentence.

The train to the airport was typically late and we missed our flight by half an hour.

Another way of showing what you think, is to use **to be** before an adjective.

To be fair, she's only been in the job five minutes – we ought to give her a chance.
To be frank, if you don't work harder, you won't pass your exam.
To be honest, I'd rather stay in and watch a film than go to the cinema.

You can also do this by using **to put it** followed by an adverb.

To put it bluntly, I'd rather you'd stayed at home.

Exercise 1

Match the sentence halves.

1 The baby was understandably	**a** late and went on for hours.
2 The children were amazingly	**b** frightened by all the noise.
3 The show was disappointingly	**c** poorly trained and rather confused.
4 The dinner was typically	**d** reluctant to complain.
5 The new teachers were obviously	**e** short and not very funny.
6 The injured woman was unexpectedly	**f** quiet for the whole of the journey.

Exercise 2

Choose the correct word or words.

Hi Megan,

How are you? I'm OK. Well, [1]**to be honest / in my opinion / amazingly**, I'm not feeling all that great.

The thing is, since I started this course at the college, I'm not so sure it's right for me. I know I was very keen before I started and [2]**sadly / amusingly / surprisingly**, my parents agreed with me for once. [3]**Rightly / Fortunately / Generously** they could afford to pay for the course too. But now I realize I'm in the wrong place.

[4]**Apparently / Stupidly / Interestingly**, all the other students have previous experience – unlike me. I don't know why I wasn't told that it was necessary. [5]**Generally / Carelessly / Presumably** they thought I already knew.

So, I'll probably give it another week and then I may come home.

Let me know what you think.

Tom

Exercise 3

Decide if the pairs of sentences have the same meaning.

1 A Everyone was very surprised when Anna won first prize in the literary competition.
  B Amazingly, Anna won first prize in the literary competition. ❏

2 A It's odd, I know, but I've never really liked chocolate.
  B Funnily enough, I've never really liked chocolate. ❏

3 A Presumably, the thief was disturbed before he could find the jewels.
  B We have discovered that the thief was disturbed before he could find the jewels. ❏

4 A You understand, of course, that I couldn't tell the customer what had happened.
  B Obviously, I couldn't tell the customer what had happened. ❏

5 A Stupidly, I allowed the sales assistant to take my credit card into the manager's office.
  B I didn't know that the sales assistant had taken my credit card into the manager's office. ❏

Exercise 4

Write one missing word in sentence B so that it means the same as sentence A.

1 A I could well understand why Liz was so excited.
  B _____, Liz was very excited.

2 A I don't think Matthew is the right person for this job, to be frank.
  B _____, I don't think Matthew is the right person for this job.

3 A You may think it strange, but we actually prefer to sit near the back of the concert hall.
  B _____ enough, we actually prefer to sit near the back of the concert hall.

4 A No one could believe that the climbers had reached the summit in only two days.
  B _____, the climbers had reached the summit in only two days.

Exercise 5

Are the highlighted words correct or incorrect in the sentences?

1 I don't think James realized that he was breaking the law, to be **fair** ❏.

2 **According to me** ❏, that trip was a waste of time and money.

3 **To our astonishment** ❏, a car drew up outside the house and Marcus stepped out of it, wearing a very smart suit.

4 **Wisely** ❏, we decided to phone our accountant before borrowing more money.

5 The driver of the van which crashed into the bridge was not injured, **with luck** ❏.

6 There wasn't anyone famous at the party after all, **for** ❏ my disappointment.

only / hardly / scarcely / quite / very much

Adverbs to add information about situations

In this unit you learn to use adverbs to give more information about a situation.

When Alan and May decided to go for a walk in the hills, they **only** planned a day out away from their books. They were both **very much** looking forward to being outdoors as they were **quite** fed up with sitting at their desks all day. However, they had **scarcely** gone more than a kilometre when they heard shouts. They ran in the direction of the noise and discovered two young men, one of whom had fallen and hurt his leg **quite** seriously.

Adverbs to add information about situations

When you want to give more information about the extent of an action or the degree to which an action is performed (in other words, *how much*), you use adverbs of degree, for example, **only**, **hardly**, **quite**, **very**. These adverbs modify the verb: they make the verb stronger or weaker.

I **hardly** know her. (= weaker)
I'm **very** pleased to meet you at last. (= stronger)

only

The adverb **only** means **no more / other than**. You usually put **only** in the middle position in a sentence (that is, after the auxiliary verb and before the main verb).

I've **only** been to Italy once.
Jenny **only** attended the last five minutes of the meeting.

You can often put **only** before a noun phrase, especially a number or quantity.

She works **only** on Saturdays.
He gets **only** a small salary for the work he does.

You can put **only** at the beginning of a sentence before a noun phrase, too.

> **Only** coffee is served here.
> **Only** the manager can offer discounts to customers.

You can also use **only** as an adjective.

> The **only** thing you can do now is apologize.
> My **only** mistake in the interview was forgetting to tell them about my specialist qualifications.

hardly

The adverb **hardly** means **scarcely** or **almost not at all**. You put **hardly** before the main verb.

> I **hardly** recognized you, you've grown so tall!
> Beth could **hardly** walk by the end of her training session.

You use **scarcely** in the same way.

> He **scarcely** takes the dog for a walk – it's always down to me.
> I **scarcely** go swimming. I find it very boring.

You can also use **hardly/scarcely** with **any**, **at all** and **ever**.

> Tina loves riding her horse but she **hardly ever** has time.
> I've **hardly** spoken to **anyone** today.

> A How well do you know David?
> B Oh, **hardly at all**.

Remember!

Don't confuse **hardly** with **hard**.
Compare:
She works **hard**
with
I **hardly** ever go out at the weekend.

---

quite

The adverb **quite** is halfway between **very** and **not at all** in meaning. You can use **quite** before an adjective or adverb, or before a main verb or noun phrase.

> My grandma's **quite old** now so she stays at home a lot.
> I go dancing **quite often**.
> Mel **quite likes** Steve.
> There were **quite a lot of people** at the pool.

very much

The adverb phrase **very much** means **to a high degree** (in other words, **a lot**). You use **very much** before state verbs such as **fear, regret, doubt, look forward to, suspect.**

*I **very much doubt** we'll be home before dark.*
*Andrew **very much regrets** not buying that car!*
*Jade is **very much looking forward to** her birthday party.*

Exercise 1

Match the two parts.

1	I was hardly	**a**	expected a brief tour, not a three-hour inspection.
2	We very much	**b**	dressed when the phone rang again.
3	We had only	**c**	regretted the decision to leave the group.
4	I had scarcely	**d**	understand that you need time to think about this.
5	I quite	**e**	begun cooking when the guests arrived.
6	They were quite	**f**	interesting paintings, but not of the quality we had expected.

Exercise 2

Put each sentence into the correct order.

1 to find out / wanted / the old lady / what / the man only / was doing / .

_____

2 when we / scarcely entered / had to / we had / the club / leave / .

_____

3 I / that I / helped him / very much / ever / regret now / .

_____

4 was so confused / that he / what / hardly knew / he / to say / .

_____

5 prefer squash / enjoy tennis, / I really / quite / but / I / .

_____

6 losing / was / a disaster / a good customer / quite / such / .

_____

Exercise 3

Which sentences are correct?

1 When I heard the news I knew hardly what to say. ❑

2 This isn't really my kind of music, to be honest. ❑

3 It's quite a comfortable old chair, only it does need a bit of a clean. ❑

4 We scarcely opened the door when we heard a terrific crash in the road. ❑

5 I very much suspect that we will never hear from that company again. ❑

6 That's the best party I've been to for ages, especially the music, which was quite good. ❑

Exercise 4

Decide if the pairs of sentences have the same meaning.

1 A Your new printer probably won't arrive today.
  B I very much doubt whether your new printer will be delivered today. ☐

2 A Are you sure you want to buy that top? Because it is quite expensive, you know.
  B Are you definitely going to buy that top? You do realize it's extremely expensive, ☐ don't you?

3 A An email stating that you accept the terms of the contract will be quite acceptable.
  B It's perfectly OK to send an email accepting the terms of the contract. ☐

4 A We received a fantastic order a few years after we started our business.
  B We'd scarcely got the business up and running when we got this fantastic order. ☐

5 A I only got an appointment to see the great man by pretending to be someone else.
  B I had to pretend to be someone else in order to get an appointment to see the great ☐ man.

Exercise 5

Are the highlighted words correct or incorrect in the sentences?

1 I **very much** ☐ fear the weather is about to change for the worse.

2 Michael can help you with your chemistry revision. He **hardly** ☐ studied the subject for several years.

3 Excuse me, I'm not feeling **quite** ☐ well. May I sit down?

4 This course is for **only** ☐ postgraduate students and research assistants.

5 We **scarcely** ☐ ever eat in restaurants these days because it's become so expensive.

6 We had **quite** ☐ a pleasant evening at Jane's house, but I wouldn't want to spend all my time with her.

11

Mixed conditionals

Clauses to talk about conditional situations

In this unit you learn to talk about situations and their consequences, using mixed conditionals.

You use conditional clauses to talk about a possible situation and its consequences. You use conditionals to

- talk about a situation that sometimes exists or existed:
    *If you **forget** your passport, you **can't check in** for a flight.*

- talk about a situation you know does not exist:
    *If I **had** more money I'**d buy** a better car.*

- talk about a situation when you don't know whether it exists or not:
    *I don't know why they **closed** the road, **unless** it **was** because of flooding.*

- talk about a situation which may exist in the future:
    *Don't insist on bringing Nicola **if** she **doesn't want** to come.*

if or *unless*

You can use **if** or **unless** with conditional clauses.

if

You use **if** to say that a consequence of something happening would be that something else would happen.
    *If you **brought** me breakfast in bed, I'**d love** you forever!*

unless

You use **unless** to mean **except if**.
    *You won't get far in life **unless** you're prepared to work hard.*

Verb forms in conditionals

You use different verb forms with different conditionals, to show different meanings.

Zero conditional

You use the zero conditional to say that something is generally true. In the zero conditional, you use the present simple in both clauses.
    *If/When you **travel** first class, it'**s** much more comfortable.*

First conditional

You use the first conditional to say something is a real possibility. In the first conditional, you use **will** + *infinitive* with the present simple. You use the first conditional when you are thinking about the future.

> *If it's sunny tomorrow, I'll go to the beach. (= I think there is a real possibility that it will be sunny tomorrow.)*

Second conditional

You use the second conditional to say there is not a real possibility of something. In the second conditional, you use **would** or **should** with the past simple. You also use the second conditional when you are thinking about the future.

> *If I **married** a millionaire, I'd **buy** lots of expensive clothes! (= I don't think there is a real possibility that I will marry a millionaire.)*

Third conditional

You use the third conditional to talk about something in the past that didn't happen. In the third conditional, you use **would have** or **should have** with the past perfect. You use the third conditional to say that the condition and result are impossible now.

> *If I'd **known** you were coming, I'd **have bought** some cakes!*

Mixed conditional verb forms

You can mix the verb forms of conditionals when you are talking about **unreal** conditions.

Past and present

> *If I **had studied** harder at school, I **would have** a better job now. (But I didn't study hard in the past and I don't have as good a job now.)*
> *If Gary **hadn't come down with** flu, he'd **be** here at the conference. (But he did come down with flu so he isn't at the conference now.)*

Past and future

> *If I'd **managed** to get time off, I'd **be going** on holiday with you! (But I didn't manage to get time off, so I'm not coming on holiday with you.)*
> *If Ben **hadn't spent** all his money, he **would be able to** buy a present for his friend. (But Ben did spend all his money so he can't buy a present for his friend.)*

Present and past

> *If I **had** loads of money, I **would have bought** you that watch you liked. (But I don't have loads of money so I didn't buy you that watch you liked.)*
> *If I **spoke** Spanish better I **would have helped** you with your translation. (But I don't speak Spanish very well so I didn't help you with your translation.)*

Present and future

> *If I **didn't have** so much free time I **wouldn't watch** that film with you later – it sounds awful! (But I do have free time so I will watch that film with you later.)*
> *If Carla **weren't** so kind, she **wouldn't be giving** you a piano lesson this evening. You never practise. (But Carla is kind so she will be giving you a piano lesson this evening.)*

Future and past

*If I **wasn't** away on business next week, I**'d have agreed** to come with you to the hospital. (But I am away next week so I didn't agree to come with you to the hospital.)*
*If my friends **weren't visiting** this weekend, I **would have planned** for us to go away. (But my friends are visiting this weekend so I didn't plan for us to go away.)*

Future and present

*If I **were going** to my friend's tonight, we **would play** computer games. (But I'm not going to my friend's tonight so we won't play computer games.)*
*If Sean **were working** tomorrow, he **wouldn't be** with us now. (But Sean isn't working tomorrow so that's why he's with us now.)*

Conditionals with modals other than *will/would*

You often use the modals **will** and **would** in conditionals. However, you can also use other modal verbs like **could**, **might** or **may**.

*I **could** explain what happened if you'd listen to me!*
*If she hadn't wanted to come shopping, she **might** have told us.*
*If we phone now, we **may** just get some tickets for the concert.*

Exercise 1

Which sentences are correct?

1 Her new book might be a bestseller, if it will get enough publicity. ❑
2 If you've finished eating, we can leave in about ten minutes' time. ❑
3 If we take the next train, we should still arrive in time for the concert. ❑ ❑
4 We can get into the science museum for free if you'd looked for your pass. ❑
5 If I became rich, I'd given up work. ❑
6 I might call the restaurant and book a table if you've still got their number. ❑

Exercise 2

Complete the sentences by writing one word or phrase in each gap.

| has signed | hadn't bought | didn't go | has taken | would hurry up |
| knows | wouldn't have fallen over |

1 If people were more considerate, the woman _____ in the supermarket.
2 We can't start rehearsals of the play unless everyone _____ their contract.
3 I'm sure Tom would be much happier if he _____ a car in such poor condition.
4 If Sarah _____ how much swimming means to her son, why didn't she let him take part in the competition?
5 She isn't qualified for the job, unless she _____ the relevant exams without telling me.
6 If Catherine _____ with her homework, she could watch TV for an hour.

Exercise 3

Are the highlighted words correct or incorrect in the sentences?

1 If you **didn't do** ❑ everything in such a rush, you wouldn't have broken that vase.

2 If the Government knows what it's doing, far fewer people **lost** ❑ their jobs.

3 These trees **might have been chopped down** ❑ if we hadn't worked hard to save them.

4 I'd buy the plane tickets if **you'd give** ❑ me a cheque for yours.

5 Unless there are any questions, **we'd finish** ❑ now.

6 If he'd told me he didn't have much food in the house, I **could have done** ❑ his shopping at the same time as mine.

Exercise 4

Choose the correct word or words.

1 What's the worst that could happen if you **don't tell / hadn't told** your boss your computer password?

2 Who do you think **shall / should** replace you if you leave your job?

3 Could you get a new job easily if the company you work for **had gone / went** out of business?

4 You might not get a pay rise if your boss **doesn't know / hasn't known** how hard you work.

5 If your boss really appreciated your efforts, you **weren't / wouldn't have been** overlooked for promotion.

6 If your company is such a good employer, why **didn't they pay / hadn't they paid** for your computer training?

Exercise 5

Decide if the pairs of sentences have the same meaning.

1 **A** We can afford a holiday abroad because we didn't buy a brand new car.
  B If we'd bought a brand new car, we wouldn't be able to afford a holiday abroad. ❑

2 **A** I couldn't possibly face Sharon again if you haven't explained why I behaved as I did.
  B I couldn't possibly face Sharon again unless you explain why I behaved as I did. ❑

3 **A** Your mobile phone will soon run out of credit, unless you topped it up when you went shopping.
  B If you didn't top up your mobile phone while you were shopping, it'll soon run out of credit. ❑

4 **A** If your children weren't so noisy, I'd have visited you far more often.
  B I haven't visited you very often because your children used to be so noisy. ❑

5 **A** You should only go out if you tell your parents where you're going.
  B You should tell your parents where you're going before you go out. ❑

12

Expressions for interpreting past actions

might have, could have, etc.

In this unit you learn to make deductions and speculations about situations in the past.

Expressions for interpreting the past

You use modals in the present to say how certain you are about something.

*That **must be** Charlotte's new car! It's nice, isn't it? (= I'm sure that's Charlotte's car.)*
*It **can't be** Tim. He's got short hair. (= I'm sure it isn't Tim.)*

You can also use modal verbs to say how certain you are about something in the past. You use modals to make **deductions** (reaching a conclusion by reasoning) and **speculations** (forming a conclusion from incomplete evidence).

● *deduction*

*You **can't have seen** Peter because he's staying with his aunt in London.*
*It **must have been** Felicity who told her my secrets.*

● *speculation*

*You never know, Michelle **might have made** dinner by the time we get home.*
*He **could have stolen** the car while we were asleep. I guess we'll never know.*

You use modals in the present with the infinitive without **to**.

*I **can't go out** because I've got too much to do.*

When you use modals in the past, you use the modal + the perfect infinitive (**have** + *past participle*).

*He **must have done** the washing-up while we were out.*

must + perfect infinitive

You use **must** + *perfect infinitive* when you are certain about something in the past.

*I can't find Sandra – she **must have gone** home early. (= I'm certain Sandra's gone home because she isn't here now.)*
*You **must have posted** the card yesterday when you went down town. (= I'm certain you posted the card yesterday because it isn't here now.)*

might/may/could + **perfect infinitive**

You use **might/may/could** + *perfect infinitive* when you think something is possible but you aren't certain.

> *Caroline's usually here before now. She **might have got caught** in traffic.*
>
> *A Where do you think my glasses are?*
> *B You **could have left** them at the gym.*
>
> *A Where's Mick?*
> *B He **may have gone** for lunch if he isn't in his office.*

can't + **perfect infinitive**

You use **can't** + *perfect infinitive* when you are certain that something didn't happen in the past.

> *I **can't have left** my bag on the bus because I had it when I got home.*
> *You **can't have told** him not to come because he's walking up to the door right now!*

Exercise 1

Choose the correct phrase to fill each gap.

1 You **might have won / can't have won** the lottery – quick, check your numbers again!

2 You **must have finished / can't have finished** that book so soon – it's got 400 pages.

3 That **must have been / can't have been** Peter you saw in town – he's away on holiday.

4 You **must have left / can't have left** your keys in the car – they're not in the house.

5 Do you think that boy **can't have picked up / could have picked up** your book by mistake?

6 We **could have bought / couldn't have bought** a house in Madrid if we'd had a bit more money.

Exercise 2

Put each sentence into the correct order.

1 in / written / couldn't / that / French / I / have / .

_____

2 the / bus / have / to / taken / must / Ron / work / .

_____

3 accident / caused / might / the / have / rain / the / .

_____

4 might / decided / home / she / to / have / go / early / .

_____

5 chosen / couldn't / better / have / you / course / a / .

_____

6 have / the / apartment / wrong / postman / the / to / the / delivered / must / letter / .

_____

Exercise 3

Are the highlighted words correct or incorrect in the sentences?

1 He could have **gone** ❑ to university in the UK but he chose to go in the USA.

2 Can she have **forget** ❑ about our meeting?

3 I thought you must **have** ❑ left the TV on.

4 It must **had** ❑ snowed during the night.

5 She might have **felt** ❑ sick and gone home.

6 Sorry, I must **to** ❑ made a mistake.

Exercise 4

Write the correct form of the verb in brackets to complete each sentence.

1 She _____ (must / work) all night because she's finished the report.

2 You _____ (can / see) Julia in the park because she's on holiday in Greece.

3 You _____ (could / phone) me; I've been waiting for ages.

4 They _____ (might / go) shopping but I'm really not sure why they aren't at home now.

5 Oh no! I _____ (must / have) the letter; it's still here on the table.

6 Paul's got a new car. He _____ (must / get) a new job.

Exercise 5

Which sentences are correct?

1 It might have been better to go by train instead of driving. ❑

2 You can't have lock the door because it was open when I got home. ❑

3 Where might have you put your mobile phone? ❑

4 It can have been easy for them, living in such poor conditions. ❑

5 Jack must have come home very late because he's still in bed now. ❑

6 You could have tried harder to be friends with her. ❑

Exercise 6

Find the wrong or extra word in each sentence.

1 The burglar can't have to got in through this window because it's too small.

2 Tina's not here, she must have already had gone.

3 They must have been missed the bus.

4 Do you mean you might you have eaten something bad?

5 He might not have listened to got your phone message yet.

6 I couldn't have not managed without you.

13

Modals in the past
Modals for commenting on past actions

should have / needn't have, etc.

In this unit you learn to comment on past actions, using **should have**, **ought to have**, **needn't have** and **didn't need to**.

Modals for commenting on past actions

should and ought to + perfect participle

You use **should** + *perfect participle* to say that you expected something to happen but it didn't happen in the past.

> You **should have finished** your homework by now. (= I expected you to have finished your homework by now but you haven't.)
> Miguel **should have told** me by now if he was coming to the party. (= I expected Miguel to have told me by now if he was coming to the party but he hasn't.)

You use **ought to** + *perfect participle* in the same way as **should**. They have the same meaning but **ought to** is a bit more formal.

> You **ought to have been promoted** by now. (= I expected you to have been promoted before now but you haven't been.)
> They **ought to have finished** building the new bridge by now. (= I expected them to have finished building the new bridge by now but they haven't.)

> *Remember!*
>
> Note that you don't usually use the negative form of **should/ought to** + *perfect participle* with this meaning.
> You don't say ~~They ought not to have decorated the hall by now~~; ~~She should not have tidied her room by now~~.

You can also ask questions using **should** or **ought to** + *perfect participle*.

> **Do you think we should have phoned** to see how she was?
> **Ought I to have invited** your granddad for lunch?

needn't have vs *didn't need to*

You use **needn't have** + *past participle* to say that someone did something which wasn't necessary. Usually you are implying that the person didn't know at the time that they did the action that it wasn't necessary.

> You **needn't have bought** me anything but it's very kind of you.
> I **needn't have bothered** tidying the house – look at the mess it's in!

You use **didn't need to** to say that something wasn't necessary and that it was known at the time that the action wasn't necessary.

> I **didn't need to worry** about the dog – I knew he'd be OK on his own for an hour.
> We **didn't need to cook** lunch because we went out instead.

Exercise 1

Match the sentence halves.

1 We should have packed some warmer clothes
2 You ought to have told me
3 You needn't have bought any bread,
4 I had enough money
5 Ought we to have phoned
6 Do you think I should have added more salt?

a so I didn't need to go to the bank.
b This doesn't seem very tasty to me.
c because it was cold in the mountains.
d I got some earlier this morning.
e before we came?
f the truth.

Exercise 2

Put each sentence into the correct order.

1 asked / should / your / have / I / help / for / .

_____

2 come / have / should / earlier / I / ?

_____

3 take / because / Frank / got / didn't / the / he / need / a / to / lift / bus / .

_____

4 the / put / to / in / have / ought / dishwasher / dishes / the / we / ?

_____

5 needn't / have / up / I / it / do / you / going / tidied / because / to / was / .

_____

6 worn / on / needn't / because / I / jeans / have / suit / everyone / a / had / else / .

_____

Exercise 3

Choose the correct phrase.

1 You **ought to have asked / needn't have asked** permission to go into next door's garden. Mr Kent was quite annoyed.

2 I **needn't have prepared / didn't prepare** so much food because only five people came for lunch instead of eight.

3 It's 5 o'clock. Max **should arrive / should have arrived** by now.

4 Do you think we **needn't stay / ought to have stayed** longer? It might have seemed rude to leave so early.

5 I **needn't have spent / should have spent** hours reading all that information because there's a good summary of it online.

6 Ben **shouldn't have eaten / ought to have eaten** the last cake, but he was so hungry!

Exercise 4

Decide if the pairs of sentences have the same meaning.

1 A I should have told you.
  B I ought to have told you. ☐

2 A I ought to have gone home at 12.
  B I should go home at 12. ☐

3 A We needn't have brought an umbrella.
  B We didn't need to bring an umbrella. ☐

4 A Mike should have arrived by now.
  B I thought Mike would be here by now. ☐

5 A You ought to take a break.
  B It would be a good idea for you to take a break. ☐

6 A I didn't need to copy the form.
  B I copied the form but it wasn't necessary. ☐

Exercise 5

Write the past simple form of the verb in brackets to complete each sentence.

1 You _____ (should/tell) me you were coming today.

2 We _____ (ought/contact) the police yesterday.

3 We _____ (need/make) ten copies; eight would have been enough.

4 I _____ (need/have) a second interview; they gave me the job straight away.

5 The college _____ (should/send) the course details by now.

6 The dentist _____ (ought/explain) how complicated the treatment was going to be.

14

Modals for expressing feelings about actions

will / would / dare / need

In this unit you learn to express your feelings and emotions about actions, using **will**, **would**, **dare** and **need**.

will to express irritation

You can use **will** to show that you are annoyed or impatient.

*If you **will** keep borrowing your sister's clothes, she will be annoyed, won't she?*
*He **will** keep leaving wet towels on the floor! It's so annoying!*

would to express past habit

You use **would** in a similar way to **used to**. You use **would** to talk about something that happened regularly in the past but no longer happens.

*My grandparents **would take** me to the park for a picnic every weekend.*
*She **would call** in every day on her way home from work.*

will to express willingness

You use **will** to show that you are happy to do something for someone.

*I'**ll do** the shopping if you like.*
*Linda said she'**ll book** the hotel for us.*

You can also use **will** in questions to make a request.

*Will you **help** me do my maths project later?*
*Will you **give** me a lift into town this afternoon?*
*Will you **marry** me?*

dare

You use **dare** to show proof of courage. You can use **dare** in negatives and in questions.

*I **didn't dare** tell him I'd bought another pairs of shoes.*
***Dare** I ask how much you paid for that coat?*

A I'm going to tell mum you broke the neighbour's window.
*B You **wouldn't dare**!*

You use the expression **I dare say** in positive sentences to say you think something is possible or probable.

> *I dare say you've spent all the money I gave you already? (= I think you've already spent the money I gave you.)*

need + -ing

You use **need + -ing** to say that you need to do something or something needs to be done.

> *Those bins need emptying – I'm going to ring the council.*
> *Look at the state of my hair! It needs cutting. I'll make an appointment later.*

Exercise 1

Match the sentence halves.

1 If you will use your phone so much,		**a**	I would go to my grandparents' house every summer.
2 When I was younger,		**b**	while you visit your friend in hospital.
3 I'll look after your children		**c**	of course it'll need recharging all the time.
4 How dare you		**d**	because the decorators left it in such a mess.
5 I didn't dare to interrupt		**e**	speak to me like that!
6 The flat needs cleaning		**f**	because he was on the phone.

Exercise 2

Complete the sentences by writing one word in each gap.

1 This kitchen is really dirty, it _____ cleaning right away.

2 She _____ insist on interrupting when I'm speaking. It's really irritating.

3 My grandfather _____ play chess with me every Friday when I was a child.

4 I _____ dare say anything because he looked so angry.

5 If you _____ spend every evening on the phone, it's hardly surprising it costs so much.

6 _____ you marry me?

Exercise 3

Choose the correct word.

1 My neighbour is getting on my nerves because he **will / would** keep playing really loud music.

2 My mother **used / would** read a story to me every night when I was a child.

3 I'm happy to tell you that the bank **will lend / lends** you £50,000 at 5% interest.

4 I **couldn't / didn't** dare to ask how much she'd paid for the coat.

5 **Dare / Daren't** I ask how you're getting on with your new boss?

6 Your bedroom's a mess, it needs **tidy / tidying** before you go out.

Exercise 4

Which sentences are correct?

1 If you will persist in going out without a coat, it's no wonder you have so many colds. ❏
2 I heard a strange noise but I didn't dare to go and investigate. ❏
3 Dare I to ask how you did in your exams? ❏
4 The meat needs be cut into small pieces for this recipe. ❏
5 Will you check the daily sales figures while I'm at the conference? ❏
6 We would use to pick blackberries in the forest when we were children. ❏

Exercise 5

Find the wrong or extra word in each sentence.

1 How often would you like go swimming when you were a kid?
2 Will you helping get the picnic ready while I find the beach towels?
3 I daren't to tell you what he said; you'd be furious.
4 Do you think this pasta needs to cooking a bit longer?
5 Simon will being sing that same song every morning and it drives us all mad!
6 The lawyer said the contract needs be translating into Spanish.

Exercise 6

Decide if the pairs of sentences have the same meaning.

1 **A** Terry *will* borrow my mp3 player all the time.
   B Terry borrows my mp3 player more often than I want him to. ❏
2 **A** I'll get the information for you, if you like.
   B I'm willing to get the information for you, if you want me to. ❏
3 **A** Jane would go to the cinema every week when she lived in London.
   B Jane wanted to go to the cinema every week when she lived in London, but she couldn't. ❏
4 **A** That lorry needs cleaning.
   B That lorry needs to be cleaned. ❏
5 **A** If you *will* play computer games all night, of course you're tired.
   B If you played computer games all night, you'd be tired. ❏

15

Verb + object + noun / adjective
Verbs with objects and adjectives

In this unit you learn to talk about people and things using verb + object + noun / adjective

You use some verbs **only** with an object. These verbs are called transitive verbs. Transitive verbs describe events that must – in addition to the subject – involve something or someone else. They are followed by a direct object.

*Eleanor **has** lots of **friends**.*
*They are **taking on** more **staff** at the supermarket.*

You can use many of these verbs with a wide range of objects. For example, you can **want** many things:

*Can we stop for a moment, please? I **want a rest** and some **water**.*
*Fred **wants fame** and **money**.*

Some verbs only have a limited number of objects you can use with them. For example, you can only use the verb **waste** with things you can use, such as money or time.

*It's easy to **waste food** when you live on your own.*
*Stop **wasting time** and get on with your work!*

Sometimes you want to say more about the object. You can use a noun or an adjective to do this. Here are some examples:

make
*They made the kitchen a complete **mess**.*

turn
*The dye turned the water **blue**.*

consider
*She considers him very **rude**.*

believe
*I believed him to be **kind**. He wasn't.*

presume
*By law you are presumed **innocent** until proven guilty.*

report
*They reported the boy **missing** as soon as they realized he wasn't in the garden.*

call

He called her **beautiful**!

elect

They elected him **mayor**.

send

These silent phone calls are sending me **crazy**!

Exercise 1

Match the two parts.

1	We painted	a	Bill a friend.
2	The noise sent	b	the place untidy.
3	They made	c	the house white.
4	We considered	d	the room upside down.
5	The students elected	e	her president of the union.
6	The thieves turned	f	me crazy.

Exercise 2

Put each sentence into the correct order.

1 the / in / turned / my new socks / sheets blue / wash / the / .

_____

2 the / bright / dyed / my / hairdresser / hair / red / !

_____

3 the / too / made / soup / I / spicy / .

_____

4 council / mayor / elected / me / the / .

_____

5 missing / reported / her / Janice / cat / .

_____

6 jury / guilty / the / him / found / .

_____

Exercise 3

Put the correct word in each gap.

| unhelpful | impossible | cross | a fool | stolen | green |

1 to colour something _____

2 to call someone _____

3 to make someone _____

4 to consider a task _____

5 to find someone _____

6 to report something _____

Exercise 4

Find the wrong or extra word in each sentence.

1 The students elected Jim up president.

2 I painted the room to blue.

3 She considers Ross is intelligent.

4 They called me as boring.

5 He finds the situation like funny.

6 She makes me be angry.

Exercise 5

Are the highlighted words correct or incorrect in the sentences?

1 They named **the baby** ❑ Georgina.

2 He proved **her** ❑ wrong.

3 They wished **to** ❑ him luck.

4 They left her **alone** ❑.

5 The news **sent** ❑ everyone happy.

6 Kirk reported **that** ❑ the van stolen.

Exercise 6

Which sentences are correct?

1 He wished me good morning and hurried down the road. ❑

2 The film made me be sad but I'm not sorry I saw it. ❑

3 I found the app confusing because it was out of date. ❑

4 They refused the boys entry to the club as they were under 21. ❑

5 He was presumed for dead for many years, but was eventually found alive and well. ❑

6 They called him the Uncle Jim, although he was actually a cousin. ❑

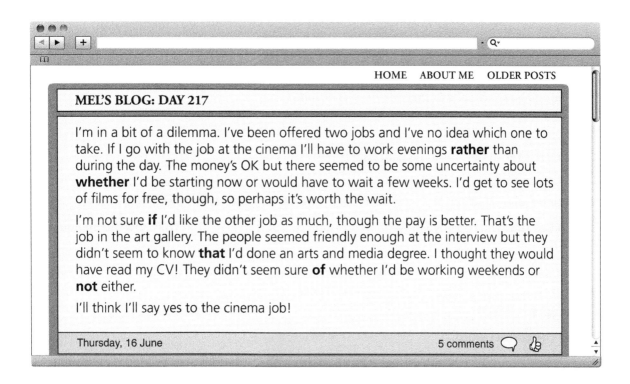# 16

Using *whether* and *that* to make statements

In this unit you learn to make factual and non-factual statements using **whether** and **that**.

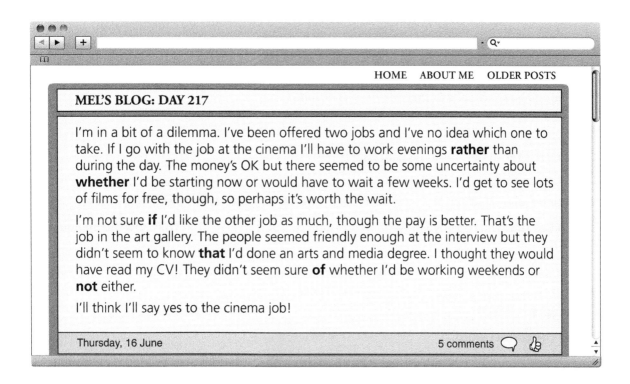

HOME   ABOUT ME   OLDER POSTS

MEL'S BLOG: DAY 217

I'm in a bit of a dilemma. I've been offered two jobs and I've no idea which one to take. If I go with the job at the cinema I'll have to work evenings **rather** than during the day. The money's OK but there seemed to be some uncertainty about **whether** I'd be starting now or would have to wait a few weeks. I'd get to see lots of films for free, though, so perhaps it's worth the wait.

I'm not sure **if** I'd like the other job as much, though the pay is better. That's the job in the art gallery. The people seemed friendly enough at the interview but they didn't seem to know **that** I'd done an arts and media degree. I thought they would have read my CV! They didn't seem sure **of** whether I'd be working weekends or **not** either.

I'll think I'll say yes to the cinema job!

Thursday, 16 June   5 comments

whether

You can use **whether** in conditional clauses which express alternative conditions. The meaning is similar to **if**.

> *I didn't know **whether** to go to the party or not. (= I didn't know if I wanted to go to the party or if I didn't want to go to the party.)*

In the example above, the two alternatives are linked with **whether** and **or not**. You don't always have to use **or not**, though the meaning is the same.

> *She asked me **whether (or not)** I wanted something to drink.*
> *He wasn't sure **whether Jane was married (or not)**.*

You use **whether** in this way when you aren't sure of the answer.

whether rather than *if*

Sometimes you use **whether** rather than **if**. In the following examples, you can use either because the meaning is the same:

> *The waiter asked us **whether/if** we wanted dessert.*
> *Vera wasn't sure **whether/if** she wanted to go to the gym.*

However, in some cases you can only use **whether**, for example, after prepositions.

> *There was a lack of information **about whether** the trains would be cancelled or not.*
> *There was some uncertainty **over whether** Dana would become the new sales manager.*

You use **whether** rather than **if** when you continue the sentence with an infinitive with **to**.

> *Barry wasn't sure **whether** to retire or not. (NOT ~~Barry wasn't sure if to retire or not.~~)*

You also use **whether** where the clause is the subject or complement.

> ***Whether** you want to or not, you're coming to visit your aunt this afternoon.*
> *She had to go to school **whether** she liked it or not.*

that

You can use **that** to talk about facts in statements.

> *Mike was sure **that** he had locked the front door – so why was it wide open?*
> *She didn't know **that** she had won the lottery until she saw the winning numbers on TV.*

You can use **that** with positive or negative sentences. You can also omit **that** and the meaning stays the same.

> *Dad thought **that** Mum had gone out shopping. (= Dad thought Mum had gone out shopping.)*

Exercise 1

Choose the correct word.

Frank edged along the clifftop, unsure ¹**that / whether** the ground would hold him or crumble under his weight, plunging him into the sea below. He had no way of knowing ²**whether / that** Logan was still lying in wait for him, maybe behind the rocks a short distance ahead, or if he had been a victim of the rock fall. He was unaware ³**that / if** Logan had already been arrested and taken to the local police station, but that was the case: Logan was a spent force, as far as Frank was concerned. ⁴**If / Whether** Frank fell to his death from the clifftop or not, Logan would play no further part in his fate.

Frank stopped for a moment, wondering ⁵**if / that** he should make a run for it, away from the cliff edge, but feared he would be too exposed. In the end, he decided to run, realizing ⁶**that / whether** it was his only hope of survival.

Exercise 2

Choose the correct word.

1 Paulina didn't realize **whether / that** Pete was waiting in the car.

2 **If / whether** you ask me, he doesn't understand what to do!

3 Martina was unsure about **whether / if** she should go on the trip.

4 Ted was told to leave the classroom, **whether / if** he wanted to or not.

5 I didn't know **if / whether** to laugh or cry.

6 Richard was sure **if / that** he wanted to travel the world after university.

Exercise 3

Which sentences are correct?

1 We have to go out, whether it's sunny or whether not. ❑

2 We need to discuss the question of if we're going to change these plans. ❑

3 Stuart wasn't sure whether he liked Sheila. ❑

4 Carmel didn't know that her friends were planning a surprise party for her. ❑

5 Let's make a decision about if we re-elect the chairman or not. ❑

6 Whether she felt ill or not, she had to go to work. ❑

Exercise 4

Decide if the pairs of sentences have the same meaning.

1 **A** Gill had to apologize whether she wanted to or not.
  B Gill didn't want to apologize but she had to. ❑

2 **A** Gareth was unaware that Helena liked him.
  B Gareth didn't know that Helen liked him. ❑

3 **A** Jack didn't know whether his design would make it into the exhibition.
  B Jack hoped his design would be accepted into the exhibition. ❑

4 **A** There was some uncertainty over whether the new sports centre would be finished by the deadline.
  B Nobody knew if the new sports centre was going to be finished on time or not. ❑

5 **A** Sheena still doesn't know if Martin is taking part in the competition.
  B Martin hasn't told Sheena whether he's joining in the competition or not. ❑

Exercise 5

Complete the sentences by writing one word in each gap.

1 Don was sure _____ resigning from his job was the right decision.

2 Bruce wasn't sure about _____ he should admit his mistake or not.

3 _____ you like hospitals or not, it's important to visit friends who are ill.

4 I'll clean the car later _____ I have time but I'm very busy today.

5 _____ you're in favour of the new town or not, you should still listen to the arguments for and against!

6 I didn't realize _____ your sister was a police inspector.

Reporting with passives

Using passives to report information

be + past participle

In this unit you learn how to report information using reporting verbs and the passive.

Missing penguin found!

A woman who reported her pet penguin missing is **expected** to be fined for keeping hold of a stolen zoo animal. It is **believed** that her nine-year-old son brought the penguin home with him after a school visit to the zoo. It is **understood** that the boy had smuggled the penguin into his school bag when the teacher's back was turned.

The penguin, which was discovered on the bank of a nearby river early this morning, was **found** to be in good health and has been returned to the zoo. The zoo said that the penguin had been **declared** missing by one of the keepers soon after the school group had left, but enquiries into its whereabouts had led nowhere.

A spokesperson for the zoo says that they hold no bad feeling towards the boy or his mother and it has been **reported** that the penguin suffered no ill effects as a result of his adventure.

If you want to show or suggest that something is an opinion which is held by an unspecified group of people, you can use a passive form or a reporting verb with **it** as the impersonal subject.

It is expected that the jury will give their verdict later this afternoon.
It was said that over a billion dollars was spent on the project.

> ### Remember!
>
> You form the passive with the correct form of the verb **be** + *past participle*.

Here is a list of reporting verbs that are used in the passive with **it** as their subject:

accept	estimate	recommend
acknowledge	expect	record
admit	explain	mention
agree	fear	note
allege	feel	notice
announce	find	object
argue	foresee	remember
assert	forget	report
assume	guarantee	request
believe	hold	reveal
claim	hope	rule
comment	imply	rumour
concede	know	say
conclude	observe	state
confirm	predict	stipulate
consider	propose	suggest
decide	realize	suppose
decree	recall	think
discover	reckon	understand

This structure is similar to a structure which uses a passive reporting verb and a **to**-*infinitive* clause. In this structure you put the main person or thing involved in the reported opinion as the subject of the reporting verb.

*A **little knowledge** is said to be a dangerous thing.*
*It is assumed that **more weight** equals more strength.*
***She is believed** to have left the country in a hurry.*

Note that the **to**-*infinitive* is usually **be**, **have** or a perfect infinitive.

Here is a list of reporting verbs from the list above that are also used in this structure:

agree	feel
allege	find
assume	guarantee
claim	hold
consider	know
discover	observe
estimate	think
expect	understand

Exercise 1

Write the passive form of the verb in brackets to complete each sentence.

1 When we began the experiment the results _____ (expect) to be better than this.

2 It _____ (believe) that the present rate of climate change is likely to continue for a long time.

3 Walter _____ (find) to be cheating and had to leave the competition.

4 My ticket _____ (declare) invalid for the train I was travelling on.

5 Since her marriage, my sister _____ (refer) to as Mrs Thomas.

6 It _____ (expect) that the cost of the new development will be in the region of $50 million.

Exercise 2

Put each sentence into the correct order.

1 been / vote / invalid / has / declared / the / .

_____

2 the / to / was / thought / brother / man / Seth's / be / .

_____

3 was / the / found / be / accountant / to / clients' / money / stealing / .

_____

4 is / be / expected / the / to / manager / held / responsible / .

_____

5 to / is / estimated / $5,000 / the / be / cost / .

_____

6 that / was / it / believed / win / Beatrice / would / .

_____

Exercise 3

Decide if the pairs of sentences have the same meaning.

1 A The theatre production has been referred to in the media as the greatest show on earth.
  B The media have exaggerated the success of the theatre production by calling it the greatest show on earth. ❑

2 A It has been calculated that around 12,000 people have applied to take part in the marathon.
  B Applications for the marathon already exceed 12,000. ❑

3 A The fire was believed to have been started by a schoolboy. ❑
  B People think that a schoolboy started the fire.

4 A It is understood that the park will be closed for a fortnight. ❑
  B The park is likely to open again in two weeks.

Exercise 4

Write the missing words in sentence B so that it means the same as sentence A.

1 A Someone suggested hiring a bus to take us to the wedding.

B It _____ that a bus should be hired to take us to the wedding.

2 A Jeremy Wallace was declared the winner of the singing competition.

B The winner of the singing competition _____ Jeremy Wallace.

3 A It is understood that Abdul is making a good recovery after his accident.

B Abdul is _____ a good recovery after his accident.

4 A People thought the house was built 100 years ago.

B The house _____ 100 years ago.

Exercise 5

Are the highlighted words correct or incorrect in the sentences?

1 Mary **considered to be** ❑ the best runner in school.

2 Quentin **was found to have lied** ❑ about his qualifications.

3 The company's chief executive **was referring to as** ❑ the Ice Queen.

4 It **used to be believed** ❑ that the world was flat.

5 The trial was **reported as being** ❑ one of the most interesting for years.

6 The results **are expected to be publishing** ❑ on Thursday.

Exercise 6

For each sentence, tick the correct ending.

1 He refused to comment on the speculation,

❑ but it is understood that an announcement will follow in the next two weeks.

❑ but it understood that an announcement will follow in the next two weeks.

2 Doctors advise pregnant women to be careful what medication they take because

❑ they are known to harm the growing baby.

❑ it is known that drugs can harm the growing baby.

3 Many cancers

❑ are thought to be related to diet.

❑ is thought to be related to diet.

4 They carried on discussing the issue all afternoon,

❑ even though it accepted that it would be difficult to reach agreement.

❑ even though it was accepted that it would be difficult to reach agreement.

5 We know very little about him,

❑ but he is believed to have lived in the sixth century BC.

❑ he believes he lived in the sixth century BC.

Using adjectives to talk about habits, expectations and obligations

be / get used to, be supposed / bound to, had better (not), (not) supposed to, be bound to

In this unit you learn to talk about habits, expectations and obligations using **be/get used to**, **had better**, **be supposed to** and **be bound to**.

| To: Liz Thomas |
| From: Beth Thomas |
| Subject: Hello! |

Hi Mum

I hope you're well. I'm really sorry – I know I was **supposed** to email you last week but so much has been going on, there hasn't been enough time.

As I feared, coming to China has been a bit of a culture shock. The most difficult thing to **get** used to is the food. It's so different to what we eat in Britain. A lot of it is delicious, but sometimes I have no idea what I'm eating.

Business etiquette also takes a bit of getting used to. For example, when a business person gives you their card, you're **supposed** to accept it with two hands and study it carefully before putting it away. I keep forgetting and I'm worried that I've offended someone.

The weather has also been a bit of a surprise. It's really hot here. On the first day, I tried to walk from my hotel to a restaurant. Halfway there, I had to stop and hail a taxi because I was so hot. I think in the future I **had** better avoid walking anywhere!

Some things aren't so alien though. I'm already used to **living** in my apartment here. It's lovely and modern like my apartment at home and there's a great view over Beijing.

I normally adapt to new environments very quickly, so I think I'm **bound** to get over the culture shock soon. It would really help though, in the meantime, if you could tell me about some familiar things. I'm feeling a bit homesick!

Love
Beth

---

be used to

You use **be used to** to talk about habits. If you say you **are used to** something or doing something, it means you are accustomed to a situation or habit.

*I'm **used to** getting up early. I've been doing it for years.*
*She's **used to** the kids being so noisy.*

You can make **be used to** negative to talk about something or doing something that you are not accustomed to.

*Karl **isn't used to** spending time on his own.*
*My parents **aren't used to** having so much free time now they're retired.*

> *Remember!*
>
> Don't confuse **be used to** with **used to** which you use to talk about habits in the past, for example, *I used to go running every morning (but I don't any more).*

get used to

You use **get used to** to talk about becoming used to something or doing something.

*I don't like my new job but I'll have to **get used to** it.*
*It was scary at first but I've **got used to** being at high school now.*

You can make **get used to** negative to talk about the fact that you are not able to become accustomed to something or doing something.

*I **can't get used to** this new computer system no matter how hard I try.*
*Nina **can't get used to** living in Italy – she says it's so different from home.*

had better (not)

You use **had better (not)** to say that something is the right thing to do. You can use **had better not** with **I** or **we** to show an intention. You use it with **you** to give advice or a warning.

*I'**d better tell** the teacher why I haven't done my homework.*
*You'**d better not admit** you overheard that conversation.*
*We'**d better meet** to discuss the situation.*
*You'**d better go** before I get angry.*

(not) supposed to

You use **(not) supposed to** to talk about expectations and obligations.

*You'**re supposed to** have arrived an hour ago!*
*Shh! You'**re not supposed to** make any noise after midnight.*

You use **(not) supposed to** with the verb **be**.

be bound to

You use **be bound to** to say that you are sure about a situation or about something that will or will not happen.

> He's **bound to** be late. He loves keeping everyone waiting.
> They're **bound not to** have realized we're away. They never listen.

Exercise 1

Choose the correct word or words.

1 When he first moved to the city, Scott thought that he would never **be used to / get used to / used to** the noise of the traffic at night.

2 **Hadn't / Wouldn't / Shouldn't** you better finish your homework before you watch TV?

3 You **better had / had better / had better not** go swimming so soon after eating – it's dangerous.

4 The groom **not supposed / is not supposed / supposed** to see the bride in her wedding dress before they get married; it's bad luck.

5 With excellent qualifications like that, Nathan **bound to / isn't bound to / is bound to** land a good graduate position.

Exercise 2

Which sentences are correct?

1 I don't think I'll ever getting used to the English weather. ❑

2 I'm used to live in Italy but I moved back to the UK three years ago. ❑

3 I'd better not eat another slice of cake or I'll ruin my dinner. ❑

4 Simon's studied so hard, he's bound passing his exam. ❑

5 Oh no! The flowers have died. You were supposed to water them! ❑

6 The puppy didn't like to be left alone at first but now he's use to it. ❑

Exercise 3

Decide if the pairs of sentences have the same meaning.

1 **A** Dan was supposed to do the shopping but he forgot.
  B Dan should have done the shopping but he forgot. ❑

2 **A** Claire's bound to be nervous about performing in front of all those people.
  B Claire's really nervous about performing in front of all those people. ❑

3 **A** Alessandro is getting used to working night shifts.
  B Alessandro finds working nights really difficult. ❑

4 **A** It's getting late. I think we'd better be going home now.
  B We should be going home now. It's getting late. ❑

5 **A** I'm not used to getting up so early in the morning. It puts me in a bad mood.
  B I used to get up really early every morning. It put me in a bad mood. ❑

Exercise 4

Write the missing words in sentence B so that it means the same as sentence A.

1 A You should probably bring an umbrella in case it rains.

   B You had _____ an umbrella in case it rains.

2 A It's very likely that Scott will fail his exams this term.

   B Scott is bound _____ his exams this term.

3 A Tania should have visited her grandma yesterday but she went shopping instead.

   B Tania was _____ her grandmother yesterday but she went shopping instead.

4 A The midnight sun in Norway will always be a strange sight for me.

   B I don't think I'll ever _____ the sight of the sun at night in Norway.

Exercise 5

Write the correct form of the verb in brackets to complete each sentence.

1 Working from home was very strange at first, but Mark is gradually _____ (used to) it.

2 You _____ (had better) eat that berry. It might be poisonous.

3 Shall we go outside to talk? We _____ (supposed to) talk in the library.

4 You _____ (bound to) love New Zealand, Clive, it's absolutely beautiful!

5 Sheila _____ (supposed to) know what Wes had bought her for her birthday, but she found her present in the wardrobe by mistake.

6 I found the diet difficult at first because I _____ (used to) counting calories, but now I don't even have to think about it.

Exercise 6

For each sentence, tick the correct ending.

1 I don't mind babysitting for them
   ❑ because I used to going to bed late.
   ❑ because I'm used to going to bed late.

2 Leila is very good with children
   ❑ because she is used to looking after her younger brother and sister.
   ❑ because she gets used to looking after her younger brother and sister.

3 Pablo explained to Hazel
   ❑ that he didn't used to eating a big meal at lunchtime.
   ❑ that he wasn't used to eating a big meal at lunchtime.

4 She was surprised not to be asked her opinion
   ❑ because she was used to her boss including her in all decisions.
   ❑ because she used to her boss including her in all decisions.

5 I was shocked at what he said
   ❑ because I wasn't used to being spoken to in that way.
   ❑ because I didn't used to being spoken to in that way.

19

Future in the past

was / were to, would, was / were (not) going to, just about to

In this unit you learn to use verbs to talk about the future in the past.

was / were to

You use **was / were to** + *infinitive* when you are talking about events that were in the future at a certain time in the past.

> *This was the place where I **was to** spend my childhood.*
> *We **were to** stay in Lisbon for the next sixteen years.*

You use **was / were to** + *infinitive* to talk about things that did happen. If you want to talk about things that didn't happen, you use **was / were to have** + *past participle*.

> *This is where the meeting **was** meant **to have taken place** but they found a better venue in the end.*
> *She **was to have sent** me that information by eight o'clock but I still haven't had it.*
> ***Weren't you to have gone** swimming this evening?*

would

You can also use **would** + *infinitive* without *to* to express something that has not happened at the time in the past we are talking about.

> *He was confident that he **would get** the job.*
> *She knew she **would pass** her driving test first time.*
> *I thought they **would pick me up** but they forgot.*

was / were (not) going to

You use **was / were (not) going to** to talk about past intentions that didn't happen. You use **was / were (not) going to** with the infinitive without **to**.

> *I **was going to wash** the car but it started raining.*
> *Dee **was going to come round** for a bit but she's changed her mind.*
> *Heidi **wasn't going to let us know** she was getting married.*
> ***Weren't you going to ask** Zena to the barbecue?*

was / were (not) going to with just

You can also use **was / were (not) going to** with **just** to talk about something you were on the point of doing in the past but didn't.

*Hi, Brenda! I **was just going to phone** you!*
*I **was just going to go** to bed when Simon called round for a chat.*
*Were **you just going to throw** that away?*

> ## Remember!
>
> You can also use **was just about to** with the same meaning as **was / were going to**. For example, *Jed **was just about to** call Penelope when she turned up on the doorstep.*

Exercise 1

Match the sentence halves.

1 This was the room where I was to work
2 There was to have been a ban
3 He was sure that the tests would show
4 She was to have resigned last week
5 The conference was to have taken place at the Park Hotel
6 The judges of the talent contest knew

a that there was nothing wrong with him.
b but it was cancelled at the last minute.
c that she was to become a great actress.
d for the next three years.
e on bringing food into the office but it was never enforced.
f but she changed her mind.

Exercise 2

Put the correct word in each gap.

| bored | had | done | charged | got | hadn't | been | was |

Hey Nell,

How was your day? I wish I ¹_____ got up this morning! I woke up late because my phone had gone dead so the alarm didn't go off. If only I'd ²_____ it before I'd gone to bed. I arrived late to work and my boss wasn't very happy. It would've been OK if only I'd ³_____ able to ring and tell her what had happened. Anyway, work was so dull. No one came to Reception and I wished I ⁴_____ taken a magazine to read. It might have been better if only my colleague Michaela hadn't ⁵_____ me to death with stories about her children! I think it's time I ⁶_____ my life sorted!

M

x

Exercise 3

Decide if the pairs of sentences have the same meaning.

1 A Things would have turned out OK if Jed hadn't lied to the teacher.
   B If Jed had lied to the teacher, things would have been OK. □

2 A If only the letter had arrived this morning! □
   B I wish the letter had arrived this morning.

3 A Carmen wished she hadn't dumped her boyfriend.
   B Carmen wished her boyfriend hadn't finished with her. □

4 A Dave wished he had met Helen sooner.
   B Dave would like to have met Helen sooner. □

5 A I think it's time we went home – you're yawning!
   B I think we should go home now because you look tired. □

Exercise 4

Write the correct form of the verb in brackets to complete each sentence.

1 He _____ (wish) he was taller so he would be better at basketball.

2 If only they _____ (have) phoned before leaving – we could have told them the show was cancelled.

3 The lecture would have gone well if only Trina hadn't _____ (keep) interrupting.

4 My class was cancelled this morning – I wish I'd _____ (stay) in bed!

5 Vanessa wished her friend Martina _____ (be) a bit more confident.

6 Lulu might have been OK at climbing, if only she _____ (have) listened to the instructor.

Exercise 5

Choose the correct word.

1 It **is / was** time I grew up a bit – I need to get a job and save some money.

2 If only my brother **hadn't / had** told me he was coming round – I'd have cooked dinner for him.

3 Lena wished she'd **remembered / reminded** to ask Amy not to bring Carl to the party.

4 The meeting would have gone well if only everyone **has / had** brought their ideas to the table.

5 If only I'd downloaded the new album before I **went / gone** to the concert – I would have known the band's new tracks.

6 I wish I **hadn't / had** argued with my mum – I hate falling out with my parents.

20

Future perfect

Verbs to talk about the future in the past

In this unit you learn to use the future perfect simple and future perfect continuous to talk about things that haven't happened yet in the future; and you learn to use the present perfect continuous to talk about the present effects of something that started in the past and is still continuing.

Do you have money worries?
Get help now! Here's what one of our customers had to say about us.

'I'd been worrying about money and things were getting so bad that I had decided to see a professional adviser. She explained that I have been spending more than I earn and then she helped me plan for the future.'

By the new year, I will have been following the plan for six months. I have been finding it tough but at last I feel in control of my life and if I can keep on like this I will have paid off all my debts in two years' time.'

Future perfect simple

You use **will/shall** + **have** + *past participle* to talk about future events. You use the future perfect simple to talk about something that has not happened yet but will happen before a particular time in the future.

> *I'll have finished work for the holidays by this time on Friday!*
> *She won't have heard back from the company until next Monday.*
> *Will you have finished in the shower any time soon?!*

Note that you must include the reference to a time in the future by using an adverbial or another clause, for example:

> *by this time on Friday*
> *until next Monday*
> *soon*

Future perfect continuous

You also use **will/shall** + **have been** + **-ing** to talk about future events. You use the future perfect continuous to talk about the duration of an event at a specific time in the future.

*By the end of this week I'll **have been training** non-stop **for twelve days**.*
*The project **will have been running for six years** this May.*

Note that you must include the reference to a time in the future as well as the duration of the event (**by the end of the week ... for twelve days, for six years this May**).

Present perfect continuous

You use **have been** + **-ing** to refer to past events that have continued to the present.

*They've **been making** that noise all day – I haven't been able to concentrate. (= They started making the noise at the beginning of the day and they are still making the noise now.)*

You also use the present perfect continuous with time adverbials to talk about **how long** something has been happening (e.g. **all day**).

*I've **been waiting** to see a doctor **for hours**. (= I started waiting for the doctor hours ago and I am still waiting)*

You use the present perfect continuous when you are concerned with the present effects of something that started in the past and is still continuing. In the first example, the person is concerned that the noise is still continuing and that they can't concentrate. In the second example, the person is concerned that they are still waiting to see a doctor.

Exercise 1

Put the correct word in each gap.

| going | recovered | married | contacting | researching | discovered |

Hi Peter!

Sorry I haven't been in touch, but I've been busy recently – my parents will have been
1_____ for 25 years next year, so we are planning a big party. I've been
2_____ all their friends secretly to invite them. My brother and I have also
been 3_____ our family tree, so now I have even more people to invite! We've
4_____ family members we didn't even know existed.

Unfortunately my dad has a problem with his chest at the moment, but I'm sure he will have
5_____ by then. He's been 6_____ to a really good doctor, so it should
be fine.

Hope to see you soon,

Mollie

x

Exercise 2

Match the sentence halves.

1 We can't move in next week
2 I've been looking at health websites

3 By tomorrow, they will have been

4 I was glad when Anna decided to leave
5 I'm afraid you can't enter the concert hall
6 Next year, she will have been headteacher

a without food or water for a week.
b because she's been driving me mad with her complaining.
c because the builders won't have finished by then.
d at this school for 20 years.
e to get some advice on losing weight.
f because the show will already have started.

Exercise 3

Which sentences are correct?

1 I've been learning French for three years. ❏
2 Do you think she'll have been completing the work by Friday? ❏
3 Sam won't have told him the bad news yet. ❏
4 George will have been hoping for some better news. ❏
5 Who are these people? They will have been following us all day. ❏
6 It's possible that I might have finishing before lunch. ❏

Exercise 4

Write the missing words in sentence B so that it means the same as sentence A.

1 A I have lived in Rome for 11 months.
   B By next month I _____ in Rome for a year.
2 A Will Colin be here at 5 o'clock?
   B _____ arrived by 5 o'clock?
3 A In half an hour, our meeting will be over.
   B _____ finished our meeting in half an hour.
4 A Ariane always leaves work at 6 p.m.
   B By 6.15 p.m., _____ left work.
5 A Tim will not be able to do all the housework before he leaves.
   B _____ done all the housework before he leaves.
6 A Spain is the only European country I have never visited.
   B When I go to Spain, _____ visited every country in Europe.

Exercise 5

Choose the correct words.

1 Chloe **has tried / has been trying / will have tried** to contact you for hours.

2 They'll be exhausted if they **haven't been having / won't have had / haven't had** a break all day.

3 Do you think you **will have decided / will have been deciding / have decided** whether or not to take the job by tomorrow?

4 Marcus **has been having / will have been having / has been have** a difficult time at work recently.

5 The soldiers will need a meal, because they **had been marching / will have been marching / will be march** for six hours.

6 I'm supposed to be looking after Harry's house, but he **hasn't been leaving / hasn't left / won't have left** me a key.

Exercise 6

Put each sentence into the correct order.

1 been taking / antibiotics because / I have / chest infection / of a / .

_____

2 have been / next month / for five years / living abroad / Fiona will / .

_____

3 will have / I don't think / been approved / by May / the plans / .

_____

4 executive have / by then / been appointed / new chief / will the / ?

_____

5 behaving brilliantly / all morning / have been / both of / the children / .

_____

6 seen the / remember that / documents before / the meeting / Douglas won't have / .

_____

Exercise 7

Are the highlighted words correct or incorrect in the sentences?

1 Lara **has been written** ❏ poetry for a few years.

2 Mira **won't have cooked** ❏ enough food for all these people.

3 Have you ever **been meeting** ❏ Tina Wallis?

4 Another ten minutes and we **will have been waiting** ❏ for three hours!

5 At least Roger shouldn't be tired because he **won't have been working** ❏ that day.

6 Hopefully, we **will have deciding** ❏ what to do by then.

Exercise 8

Write the future perfect simple form of the verb in brackets to complete each sentence.

1 I'm sure that Gerry _____ (tell) Adam the news by then.

2 By then, they _____ (notice) that the money is missing.

3 I'm worried that Becky _____ (not work) hard enough to pass the exam.

4 Do you think that Olga _____ (manage) to catch the last train?

5 I gave them all the information, but I suspect they _____ (not read) it.

6 We could call Seb. He _____ (arrive) in Moscow by now.

Exercise 9

Choose the correct phrase.

Dear Grandma

By this time next Friday, I ¹**will be finishing / have been finishing / will have finished** all my exams! Do you realize I ²**have been studying / will be studying / will have studied** medicine for six years now? It ³**will be / will have been / has been** hard work!

On Friday evening I ⁴**will have been celebrating / will be celebrating / have been celebrating** with my friends, although we will probably be tired because we will ⁵**have been done / have been doing / to do** exams all week! In August I'm going to Australia for a three-week holiday. I ⁶**will be having / will have been having / will have had** my exam results by then, so I should be able to relax!

Lots of love

Lizzie

21

It's time + past simple / continuous

Clauses to express criticism and regret

In this unit you learn how to express feelings about what should or shouldn't be happening. You also learn to express criticism and regret.

It's time + past simple / continuous

You use **It's time** + past simple / continuous to

● say it's a good idea:

You use **It's time** + *past simple / past continuous* to say that something should be happening but isn't happening at the moment of speaking.

> **It's time** you **went** to bed. You look very tired.
> **It's time** we **were** going. It's very late.

● express criticism:

You can also use this structure to express criticism.

> **It's time** you **sorted** your life out!
> **It's time** we **tidied** out that storeroom – it's in a real mess.

Remember!

You can't use this structure in a negative sentence. ~~It's time you didn't go home~~.

I wish + past simple / past perfect

You use **wish** + *past simple* or *past perfect* when you want to express regret.

I wish + past simple

You use **I wish** + *past simple* to express what you want to happen now.

> **I wish** I **was** on holiday.
> **I wish** you **were** here.
> **Do** you **wish** you **had** a more interesting job?

I wish + past perfect

You use **I wish** + *past perfect* to express regret about past events.

> She **wishes** she **hadn't married** him.

*I wish **I'd taken up** gymnastics earlier.*
***Do** you **wish** you'd celebrated your birthday now?*

if only + past perfect / conditional

You can also use **if only** + *past perfect / conditional* to express regret.

if only + conditional

You use **if only** + *conditional* in a similar way to **wish** + *past simple* to express what you want to happen now.

> **If only** you **would be** quiet for a minute and let me hear myself think!
> **If only** she **could express** herself better, she'd be good at English.

if only + past perfect

You use **if only** + *past perfect* in a similar way to **I wish**, in order to express strong regret about past events.

> **If only** I **hadn't put on** weight – I'd still be able to wear my favourite jacket.
> **If only** you'd told me how you felt sooner.

Exercise 1

Which sentences are correct?

1 I wish I learned to play an instrument when I was younger. ❑
2 She wished she was so tall. If she wasn't she could've been a dancer. ❑
3 Everything would be fine if only she wouldn't keep asking questions. ❑
4 If only I'd asked her to marry me, she wouldn't have left. ❑
5 It's time I told him what I really think about the situation. ❑

Exercise 2

Are the highlighted words correct or incorrect in the sentences?

1 If only you **have** ❑ better qualifications – you'd soon get a job.
2 I wish I **could speak** ❑ English more fluently.
3 It's time you **were setting off** ❑ – you don't want to miss the train.
4 Isn't it about time Charlie **is given** ❑ his own front door key?
5 All her life Margaret has wished that she**'s had** ❑ a brother or sister.

Exercise 3

Choose the correct word or words.

1 When Tim caught Helen looking at her watch, he realized it was time he **would leave / left / had left**.
2 If only I **didn't / wouldn't / won't** have to go to work tomorrow, we could meet for lunch.
3 Marian loves London and she wishes she **would / can / could** live there.
4 If only the children **wouldn't / don't / won't** keep arguing.
5 Don't you think it's time we **move / moved / 'd moved** to a smaller flat?

Exercise 4

Write the correct tense of the verb in brackets to complete each sentence.

1 It's a month since you graduated, so isn't it time you _____ (start) to look for a job?

2 If only I _____ (not make) such a silly joke – Caroline still hasn't forgiven me.

3 It's high time the children _____ (encourage) to tidy up their room.

4 I wish my neighbours _____ (be) a bit friendlier, but at least they aren't noisy.

5 Joanna wished the room _____ (decorated) before she'd bought the new furniture.

6 If only you _____ (make) such silly jokes – no one finds them funny.

Exercise 5

Put the correct word or words in each gap.

| live | hadn't told | calls | 'd had | had | went | go | would call | lived |

Hi Anwen

Bev dropped in yesterday – without warning, as always. If only she ¹_____ me first, so I could be ready for her, but she never does. Yesterday was a particularly bad day for a visit, and on top of that I wished I ²_____ her I'd lost my job; she went on and on about it. In the end, I had to say, 'It's time I ³_____ shopping, Bev, or I won't have anything to eat this evening.' But did she take the hint? Of course not! I wish I ⁴_____ a pound for every time she ignored what she didn't want to hear. Anyway, she carried on and I began to wish I ⁵_____ the courage to close the door in her face when she arrived! At last she stood up to go, and she had the nerve to say, 'If only you ⁶_____ closer, Megan, I could see you much more often.' I really had to bite my lip!

Love

Megan

Exercise 6

Decide if the pairs of sentences have the same meaning.

1 A It's time we were going home.
   B We should have gone home. ☐

2 A If only Ben had let me know he was going shopping.
   B I wish Ben would let me know when he goes shopping. ☐

3 A It's time you were shown how to operate the alarm system.
   B I think you should be shown how to operate the alarm system. ☐

4 A Belinda wishes she hadn't made such a fuss. ☐
   B Belinda is sorry that she made such a fuss.

5 A If only you'd taken my advice. ☐
   B I wish you'd take my advice.

22

Perfect and continuous infinitives

Clauses for interpreting situations and actions

In this unit you learn how to interpret situations and actions using the perfect and continuous infinitives.

Bank robber caught!

A woman, who is now known **to have been living** in a £2 million house in London, was today found guilty of carrying out five bank robberies. She entered banks and pretended **to be working** in them. She is said **to have gone** into the banks and calmly walked through security into the staff areas. In court she said she was surprised not **to have been stopped** by the security guards and how easy it had been. Once inside the bank, she claimed **to be checking** the bank's systems and that she was from head office. She just walked out of banks with tens of thousands of pounds. She says her only regret is not **having taken** more money.

Perfect and continuous infinitives

The perfect infinitive

You use **(not) to have** + *past participle* (the perfect infinitive) to interpret a situation or action. You usually use the perfect infinitive after an auxiliary verb and after the verbs **appear** and **seem**.

> Mum **was** so pleased **to have met** your new girlfriend.
> He seems **to have disappeared**. I can't find him anywhere.
> She appears **to have forgotten** that it's our wedding anniversary.

You can also use the perfect infinitive after the verbs **believe, know, report, say, understand** and other stative verbs.

> She is not known **to have left** the country.
> He is said **to have vanished** overnight.
> They are **understood** to have robbed the bank on their way home from work.

The continuous infinitive

You can also use **(not) be / to be** + **-ing** (the continuous infinitive) to interpret a situation or action. As with the perfect infinitive, you usually use the continuous infinitive after an auxiliary verb and after the verbs appear and seem.

> *You must **be joking**!*
> *I happened **to be walking** past the shop when the fire broke out.*
> *She seems **to be having** a bad time of things.*

You can also use the continuous infinitive after the verbs **believe, know, report, say, understand** and other stative verbs.

> *They are understood **to be hiding** somewhere in London.*
> *She is said **to be fighting** the case in court.*
> *It's reported **to be raining** hard all over Europe.*

Exercise 1

Put each sentence into the correct order.

1 to / met / I'm / have / glad / so / you / .

_____

2 going / New / York / to / we / be / happen / to / soon / .

_____

3 for / be / pretended / waiting / to / a / I / bus / .

_____

4 been / to / woman / did / crying / have / seem / the / ?

_____

5 would / visited / to / I / museum / have / like / the / .

_____

6 been / have / able to / to / happy / you / help / I'm / .

_____

Exercise 2

Which sentences are correct?

1 I'd really like to be relaxing at home right now. ☐

2 He is bound to have forgot to lock the door. ☐

3 She is thought to be working in the Amazon now. ☐

4 You'd better not still be watching TV when I get home. ☐

5 I was upset that have received such harsh criticism. ☐

6 We just happened to passing and we thought we'd see if you were at home. ☐

Exercise 3

Decide if the pairs of sentences have the same meaning.

1 A She was happy to be working in Paris.
  B She was happy to have worked in Paris. ☐

2 A They pretended not to have seen us.
  B They pretended that they hadn't seen us. ☐

3 A He claimed to be earning a fortune working in IT.
  B He claimed that he had earned a fortune when he worked in IT. ☐

4 A I would like to have met John Lennon.
  B I wish I had met John Lennon. ☐

5 A She was happy to be spending more time with her family.
  B She was glad that she was spending more time with her family. ☐

6 A Would you rather be travelling alone than with me?
  B Would you prefer to have travelled alone than with me? ☐

Exercise 4

Find the wrong or extra word in each sentence.

1 He demanded to have be told the truth.

2 This book appears that to be missing a chapter.

3 Our family is believed to have be descended from an ancient Celtic king.

4 This car is guaranteed to have been passed the toughest safety checks.

5 The rock band is rumoured to have been being seen shopping in our local supermarket.

6 The nurse says my brother seems that to be feeling much better today than he was yesterday.

Exercise 5

Complete the sentences by writing one word in each gap.

1 I was so happy _____ to have been stuck in that traffic jam.

2 Would you like to _____ been promoted to Area Manager?

3 Martha's really pleased to _____ working in Rome again.

4 You're not the only one _____ be working long hours this week.

5 John appears to be _____ the time of his life in South America, judging by his latest email.

6 Did the car seem to have _____ badly damaged in the accident?

23

Group nouns

the crowd, the government, the public, etc.

In this unit you learn to use verbs and noun groups correctly.

Subject-verb agreement with group subjects

Group or *collective* nouns are nouns that appear in the singular form but represent a group of people. For example, **the crowd**, **the government**, **the public**, **the staff**.

When you talk about a group, you can use either the singular or the plural form of the verb, depending on whether you are thinking of the group as a single entity or as individuals.

Group nouns as a single entity

When you want to talk about a group as a single entity (as a collection of people), you use the singular form of the verb. You use the group noun in this way when the group is acting 'as one'.

*The government **is** reviewing its energy policy.*
***Does** the team **play** on Saturdays?*

When you want to talk about a group as individuals you use the plural form of the verb. You use the group noun in this way when you want to draw attention to the fact that there are individuals in the group.

*The staff **are** always fighting over who takes a break when.*
*The team **are** getting kitted out in new uniforms.*

> ### Remember!
>
> Be careful that the noun you are using is a group noun and not a plural noun like **the police**. For example, you don't say ~~The police is doing everything it can to prevent crime in the region escalating~~.

Double subjects

Double subjects seen as two entities

When you are talking about two subjects seen as two individuals, you use the plural form of the verb.

*Are your **mum and dad** coming to see you in the play?*
*The **boy and girl were sitting** opposite me the whole way home.*

Double subjects seen as one unit

When you are talking about two subjects as a single unit, you use the singular form of the verb.

Health and Safety isn't my responsibility.

Coordinated subjects

You can use **either ... or** and **neither ... nor** to talk about two subjects. When the subjects are singular, you use a singular verb.

Neither Jane nor Freddy knows how to use the washing machine.

If one of the subjects is singular and one of the subjects is plural, you use a plural verb.

Neither the coach nor the players know what happened.

However, you can also choose to use the singular or plural verb depending on whether you are thinking of the subject as a group or individual.

Neither the players nor the coach know what happened.
Neither the coach nor the players knows what happened.

In the first example, the verb is plural because we are thinking of the players and the coach as two entities. In the second example, the verb is singular because we are talking about the people as a whole team.

Exercise 1

Choose the correct word.

1 Bed and breakfast **was / were** very good value at £30 per night.

2 Economics **is / are** Julia's favourite subject at college.

3 Girls and boys usually **gets / get** similar results in their exams.

4 The police **is / are** determined to catch whoever did it.

5 Everyone **needs / need** to help with the tidying up.

6 Aerobics **is / are** a good way to keep fit.

Exercise 2

Complete the sentences by writing one word in each gap.

| isn't | were | are | was | aren't | is |

1 We are really pleased that gymnastics _____ included in the competition next week as everyone enjoys it.

2 Trial and error _____ always the best way to develop a product.

3 When I was at school, maths _____ my best subject.

4 _____ your brother and sister definitely coming to the show?

5 His wife and daughter _____ questioned by the police.

6 Tax and insurance _____ included in the price, unfortunately.

Exercise 3

Are the highlighted words correct or incorrect in this text?

In my opinion, health and safety [1]**is** ❑ given far too much importance in our society. Of course, it's terrible if anyone [2]**get** ❑ hurt or killed, but our Government [3]**seems** ❑ to want to eliminate all risk, which can only lead to a very boring life!

I firmly believe that the majority of people [4]**are** ❑ well able to make their own decisions. Adventure and risk [5]**is** ❑ important aspects of life, and I believe that our society [6]**need** ❑ to accept that accidents occasionally happen.

Exercise 4

Match the sentence halves.

1 As far as I can tell, clothes

2 For those who need it, board and lodging

3 The accompanying book and CD

4 I love travel, but food and accommodation

5 I sometimes think that politics

6 With online shopping, postage and packing

a sometimes adds a large amount to the price.

b seem to be the most important thing in Ella's life.

c are on display in the foyer.

d is available in the nearby town.

e often make it very expensive.

f is the only thing that interests Alex.

Exercise 5

Are the highlighted words correct or incorrect in the sentences?

1 All the crew **were** ❑ on board at the time of the accident.

2 Law and order **is** ❑ one of the most important issues in this election.

3 My mother and father **insists** ❑ that I should finish my studies.

4 The army **was** ❑ getting close to the border.

5 I think physics **are** ❑ very difficult to understand.

6 They had a better chance of winning if the enemy **were** ❑ on lower ground.

Exercise 6

Which sentences are correct?

1 Measles are a serious illness. ❑

2 The committee is going to make a decision later today. ❑

3 The team were disappointed with today's match. ❑

4 Health and safety are the responsibility of the deputy head. ❑

5 The staff is very worried about its job. ❑

6 The council has agreed to provide new play equipment. ❑

24

Phrasal verbs

In this unit you learn to use phrasal verbs correctly in sentences.

Separable phrasal verbs usually have two parts. You always use separable phrasal verbs with an object.

> I **handed** my homework **in**. (object = my homework)
> What **brought about** the changes in the law? (object = changes)

You can put the object between the verb and particle as in the first example, or you can put the object after the particle as in the second example. It doesn't matter which order you use: the meaning is the same.

However, if the object of the sentence is a pronoun, you always put the pronoun between the verb and the particle.

> She dropped **me** off outside school this morning.
> He paid **her** back as soon as he could.
> Looks like it might be raining for the match. Let's call **it** off.

You usually separate verbs and articles in this way when you are speaking rather than writing.

Note that when the noun phrase is long, you usually put it *after* the whole phrasal verb.

> We've been told to turn away **anyone who doesn't have a valid ticket**.

If the phrasal verb has three parts to it, you put the pronoun *after* the whole phrasal verb.

> I don't know why she **puts up with him**.
> They'll have to **make up for it** later.

Note that you can use phrasal verbs in different tenses in the same way as ordinary verbs.

Here is a list of common separable phrasal verbs:

break off	catch up	hang up
break up	drop off	pay back
bring about	drop out	take over
call off	hang on	write out

Here are some common three-word phrasal verbs:

catch up with	get away with	make up for
get along with	give up on	put up with

Exercise 1

For each question, tick the correct answer.

1 If you drop someone off, you
- ❏ stop being friends with them.
- ❏ give them a lift somewhere in a car.
- ❏ stop holding their hand.

2 If you bring something about, you
- ❏ cause it to happen.
- ❏ take it to a particular place.
- ❏ turn it to face the other way.

3 If you call off an event, you
- ❏ tell everyone about it.
- ❏ decide that it should not happen.
- ❏ change its name.

4 If you get along with someone, you
- ❏ walk with them.
- ❏ argue with them.
- ❏ enjoy their company.

5 If you put up with something, you
- ❏ accept it even though you do not like it.
- ❏ keep doing it.
- ❏ make sure you keep it with you.

6 If you make up for something, you
- ❏ try as hard as you can to achieve something.
- ❏ invent a story about what has happened.
- ❏ do something nice for someone to try and compensate for upsetting them previously.

Exercise 2

Put the correct word in each gap.

| away | into | out | back | up | along |

My friend Evelyn has had a terrible time with her son. He dropped [1]_____ of college after only two terms and came back home, and it has been a disaster. He's really [2]_____ motorbikes, and he leaves dirty bits of machinery all over the place. Also, he's constantly borrowing money, and he never pays it [3]_____.

To make things worse, he doesn't get [4]_____ with Evelyn's new boyfriend at all – her son is really rude to him. Things got so bad, she thought they might break [5]_____ because of it. I keep telling her she should ask her son to leave. He's an adult now, and she shouldn't let him get [6]_____ with that sort of behaviour.

Exercise 3

Complete the sentences by writing one word in each gap.

1 Can you just hang _____ a moment? I'll be there in a second.

2 David was way ahead, and I couldn't catch _____ with him.

3 I took him out for lunch to make up _____ forgetting his birthday.

4 If you can lend me £10, I promise I'll pay you _____ next week.

5 This is Alex Smith. He's taken _____ from Rob Peterson as sales director.

6 Could you drop me _____ at the station on your way into town?

Exercise 4

Choose the correct word or words.

1 She decided to break off **her course / the party / their relationship**.

2 I can write out **a song / a cheque / an essay** for him.

3 They hope to bring about **more food / education / political change** in the region.

4 I don't think she will be able to get away with **her passport / helping others / such dishonesty**.

5 She still stands by **her own money / her earlier statement / her illness**.

6 Our firm was taken over by **debts / a larger company / rising sales**.

Exercise 5

Which sentences are correct?

1 Can you drop off me at Ollie's house, please? ❑

2 I don't think she'll ever pay back the money we lent her. ❑

3 If you hang a second on, we can go together. ❑

4 She will always stand her son by, no matter what happens. ❑

5 He hung up before I'd finished talking to him. ❑

6 They had been having so many arguments, they decided to call the wedding off. ❑

Exercise 6

Complete the sentences by writing one phrase in each gap.

brought about	broke off	caught up	hung up	got away with	stood by

1 The accident _____ calls for new safety regulations.

2 I tried to talk to her but she just _____ on me.

3 He cheated in the exam and he _____ it.

4 She said that she _____ her decision to resign.

5 The two sides yesterday _____ talks.

6 Wage increases have not _____ with price rises.

25

Using *wh-* clauses as nouns

Who, which, what, why, when, where, whether, how

In this unit you learn to use *wh-* clauses as nouns.

When you want to talk about something that is not certain or definite, or about something where a choice has to be made, you can use clauses beginning with a **wh-** word (**who, which, what, why, when, where, how**).

> *Who will take over as manager* remains to be seen.
> *Which choice she'll make* is anyone's guess.
> *What she said* will remain a mystery.
> *Why she won't come me with me*, I don't know.
> *When the painting will ever get done* I really couldn't say.
> *Where my glasses have gone* I have no idea.
> *How you lifted that suitcase* I'll never know.

You use **wh-** clauses after prepositions and as the subject of verbs such as **be**, **depend** and **matter**.

> *What you get* depends on **who you are**.
> *How long I spent playing the game* doesn't matter.
> *When I visited her* isn't really important. It's the fact I visited her at all that matters.

You can also begin a clause with **whether**.

> *Whether* the camera will work now, who knows?
> *Whether* your car's broken down or not, you'll have to get to the meeting.

Structures consisting of a **wh-** word plus a **to** infinitive, which refer to a possible course of action, are used after prepositions. You don't usually use them as subjects but as objects or complements.

> *People about to retire often worry about* **what to do with their spare time**.
> *I've just bought this book on* **how to cook vegetarian meals**.

Exercise 1

Match the sentence halves.

1 I have absolutely no idea where   **a** the kids had been doing.

2 We found it behind the sofa but never discovered how   **b** is not yet clear.

3 I asked the teacher to show me what   **c** your dad's saying.

4 Whether Hamilton will be a good leader   **d** Sophie and Rick are.

5 She said she'd resigned but didn't say why   **e** it got there.

6 Noah, please listen to what   **f** she'd made that decision.

Exercise 2

Put each sentence into the correct order.

1 to / sure what / do / not / I'm / .

_____

2 never / it got / we / there / discovered how / .

_____

3 left home / why she / mystery / a / is / .

_____

4 she had / what / admit / done / did she / ?

_____

5 he didn't / you know / arrive / do / why / ?

_____

6 there / how / unclear / she got / is / .

_____

Exercise 3

Complete the text by writing one word in each gap.

I bumped into Julian's mum yesterday so I asked after Julian. I was quite shocked by her
response. She only had the vaguest idea [1] _____ Julian was staying in Crete and
how [2] _____ he'd been there. She didn't know [3] _____ he was doing
to earn money and she couldn't say [4] _____ he was coming back either. She said
he'd return after the summer, though exactly [5] _____ that means, I don't know! By
the way, do you have any idea [6] _____ he went to Crete? Does he have any friends
there?

Exercise 4

Are the highlighted words correct or incorrect in the sentences?

1 A healthy diet is really about eating sensibly. Of course, exactly **which** ❏ that means is a
matter of opinion.

2 Quite **how** ❏ the company makes a profit is unclear.

3 We've done well to reach this stage in our research. **Where** ❏ we go from here is the next
decision.

4 We may describe a child's behaviour as difficult, but **what** ❏ that word suggests depends on
who uses it.

5 We all agree the team needs a new captain but **how** ❏ would make the best captain is not
agreed.

6 I know I need to speak to my teacher, but **when** ❏ I should do it is the problem.

Exercise 5

Match the sentence halves.

1 This week, we have an exciting competition for you. For details on

2 She looked around the classroom and asked us

3 I watched the race, astonished at

4 Martha took me by the hand and led me to

5 He said he'd had business problems and gave me the details of

6 I wanted to talk about work, but Alice was more interested in

a how I'd lost so much weight.

b where her little brother was hiding.

c what we were studying.

d how quickly they all ran.

e how to enter, see page 43.

f what had happened and how much money he'd lost.

Exercise 6

Complete the sentences by writing one word or phrase in each gap.

| how | why | how many | who | which | how much |

1 The college has a really useful guide about _____ to manage your money.

2 Consumers have to make important decisions about _____ to trust with their savings.

3 People now have more choice about _____ hospital to receive treatment in.

4 It is not known exactly _____ cars were stolen from the yard, but it was over 100.

5 These medals are proof of _____ progress the country has made in athletics.

6 We know this happens, but we still have very little idea _____ it happens.

Exercise 7

Decide if the pairs of sentences have the same meaning.

1 A Who's going to win the election is anyone's guess.
  B Anyone can guess who's going to win the election. ☐

2 A How she puts up with him I don't know.
  B I don't know whether she likes him. ☐

3 A I really couldn't say which game is the best.
  B I'm not sure which game is the best. ☐

4 A She has no idea when he will be home.
  B She does not think he'll be home soon. ☐

5 A It remains a mystery why Carla left town that night.
  B Nobody knows why Carla left town that night. ☐

6 A How she manages to look after all those children I'll never know.
  B I don't know how many children she looks after. ☐

26

Relative clauses with prepositions

Using *wh-* clauses with prepositions

In this unit you learn to use *wh-* clauses with prepositions.

Eva Shapur remembered

Eva Shapur has long been a writer **for whom** I have the greatest admiration. Whilst I was in Paris, I was fortunate enough to meet Shapur's partner, Alex Morris, **with whom** Shapur had shared 36 years of her life. Morris was kind enough to show me the office **in which** the writer had laboured, the ink pen **with which** she had painstakingly written her novels, and even the books **in which** she had written them. Morris spoke at some length about Shapur's masterpiece, *Yellow Roses*, **on which** the forthcoming film, *May's Flowers*, is based.

Using *wh-* clauses with prepositions

You put the preposition after the verb when the relative pronoun (**who, which, where,** etc.) is the object of the preposition.

> *He was talking **to** someone.* → *Who was he talking **to**?*
> *She's talking **about** something but I don't know what.* → *I don't know what she's talking **about**.*

You can leave out the relative pronoun when it is the object of the preposition.

> *Who was **the man who you** were chatting with?* → *Who was **the man you** were chatting with?*
> *This is **the house which my mum** grew up in.* → *This is **the house my mum** grew up in.*

Note the difference between formal language and informal language when you are using **wh-** clauses with prepositions. This is especially the case when you use **whom** or **which**. You put the preposition before the **wh-** clause.

> *I haven't read the novel **on which** the film was based.*
> *Who was the woman **with whom** you were talking?*

Compare the formal forms above with their informal forms below:

> *I haven't read the novel **(which)** the film was based **on**.*
> *Who was the woman **(who)** you were talking **to**?*

Exercise 1

Complete the sentences by writing one word in each gap.

on | to | from | of | for | in

1 Mr Williams, _____ whom I spoke earlier, would very much like to arrange an appointment.

2 The gallery is located on the ground floor of the house _____ which the artist was born.

3 She is a colleague _____ whom I have the greatest respect.

4 Keating is thought to have been the real-life teacher _____ whom the character is based.

5 We also visited the village _____ which the actress came.

6 Mark Taylor and Peter Jones, one _____ whom I know, as it happens, featured on a radio programme last night.

Exercise 2

Match the two parts.

1 That's the novel that Jackson's film   **a** used to go to.

2 She sent me an email, which I   **b** was born in.

3 Hey, Karen, I met someone yesterday who you   **c** used to work with.

4 That's the health club that I   **d** applied for.

5 You can look round the actual bedroom that the princess   **e** was based on.

6 I didn't get that job that I   **f** replied to.

Exercise 3

Which sentences are correct?

1 I still live in the town in which I was born.   ❑

2 I still live in the town where I was born.   ❑

3 I still live in the town which I was born.   ❑

4 I still live in the town that I was born in.   ❑

5 I still live in the town where I was born in it.   ❑

6 I still live in the town that I was born.   ❑

Exercise 4

Put the correct word in each gap.

on | for | that | who | to | with

You know who Pete is – he's the guy ¹_____ Jamie shares the flat ²_____. Do you remember meeting them at the party that we went ³_____ a couple of months ago? He's really great. He's one of those friends that you can rely ⁴_____. You know he'll do exactly what he's says and if you've got a problem ⁵_____ you need to share, you can talk to him. He's someone I have a lot of time ⁶_____.

Exercise 5

Put each sentence into the correct order.

1 someone who / confide / Marie is / in / I often / .

_____

2 that I / a restaurant / rarely go / to / *Greens* is / .

_____

3 eating out / that we / can economize / is something / on / .

_____

4 working / on which / I'm currently / the project / that is / .

_____

5 problem which / relate / to / I can / it's a / .

_____

6 a colleague / on whom / I can / he's / depend / .

_____

Exercise 6

For each sentence, tick the correct ending.

1 I don't know
   ❏ what she was worrying about.
   ❏ about what she was worrying.

2 Lars didn't say
   ❏ which girl he had gone out.
   ❏ which girl he had gone out with.

3 This is the town
   ❏ in which my father was brought up.
   ❏ which my father was brought up

4 Manda introduced me to the people
   ❏ whom she had shared a house when she was a student.
   ❏ who she had shared a house with when she was a student.

5 Ali's mother asked him
   ❏ what he was writing about.
   ❏ on what he was writing about.

27

Using *wh-ever* correctly in sentences

whatever, however, whenever, whoever, whichever and *wherever*

In this unit you learn to use ***wh-ever*** in sentences.

When you want to say that something is the case but it doesn't matter which person, place, cause, method or thing is involved, you use:

whatever
however
whenever
whoever
whichever
wherever

> ***Whatever*** *you want to do is fine by me.*
> ***However*** *we get there, I don't care. We just need to get there on time.*
> *Call me **whenever** you need me.*
> ***Whoever*** *she is, I don't like her at all.*
> *You can have **whichever** one you want.*
> *I'll come and visit you, **wherever** you are.*

Remember!

Note that you don't usually use the word **whyever** because it means something slightly different. You use **whyever** when you want to emphasize **why** in questions:
Whyever *did you tell him that?*

You use **whatever** and **whichever** as either determiners or pronouns.

> ***Whatever*** *clothes you wear, wear them with confidence.*
> *Don't ask Marj about her boyfriend, **whatever** you do!*
> ***Whichever*** *way you look at it, this problem isn't going to be fixed any time soon.*
> ***Whichever*** *you choose, I'm sure it'll be fine.*

Another way you can say it doesn't matter who or what is involved is to use **no matter**.

> ***No matter what*** *I do, I never make any progress. (= I never make any progress, **whatever** I do.)*
> *I'll go with you, **no matter where** you go. (= I'll go with you **wherever** you go.)*

Formal and neutral / informal

Note that when you want to be more formal, you use **whatever**, **however**, **whenever**, **whoever**, **whichever** and **wherever** with the passive form.

*Whatever method **is used**, it is essential to proceed with caution.*
*However careful the approach, there **is** always some risk **involved**.*

Exercise 1

Match the two parts.

1 I compare all the products but generally choose

2 I've told Jamie he can invite

3 Essentially, this job has to be finished

4 It's a great place for kids because they're free to do

5 I'm reminded of Peter

6 It's a very tricky situation

a whenever I hear that song.

b whatever they want.

c whoever he wants to his party.

d whichever is cheapest.

e however you look at it.

f however long it takes.

Exercise 2

Complete the sentences by writing one word in each gap.

| whichever | however | whatever | whoever | whatever | whichever |

1 _____ I do, I can't seem to save any money.

2 You can have fruit or cheese, _____ you like.

3 _____ carefully you prepare for a rock climb, there will always be a degree of risk involved.

4 We can go on Monday or Tuesday, _____ suits you.

5 _____ happens, you know you can rely on us.

6 _____ told you that story was completely wrong.

Exercise 3

Match the sentence halves.

1 The fact is, whatever I say to Paul,

2 Whichever route we take to Madrid,

3 However much practice I do,

4 However many times I remind Jim to take his key,

5 Whenever I see Tony,

6 Whatever project he's in charge of

a I still can't pass my driving test.

b it's going to offend him.

c is always a complete disaster.

d he's wearing something new.

e he still forgets it.

f it's going to take the best part of a day.

Exercise 4

For each sentence, tick the correct ending.

1 You can spend your free time
- ❏ however you want to.
- ❏ whatever you want to.

2 Spend the money on
- ❏ however you want.
- ❏ whatever you want.

3 There are two colours and you can have
- ❏ whatever you want.
- ❏ whichever you want.

4 Don't lose these keys,
- ❏ however you do!
- ❏ whatever you do!

5 There was a huge menu and John said we could have
- ❏ whichever we wanted.
- ❏ whatever we wanted.

Exercise 5

Choose the correct word.

1 **Whatever / However** much Becca eats, she never seems to put on weight.

2 Serve the meat with rice, potatoes or **whichever / whatever** else you fancy.

3 **However / Whatever** you look at it, it's a big problem and it's not going away.

4 Customers are free to choose **whatever / whichever** of the two options they prefer.

5 I cook with organic ingredients **whatever / whenever** possible.

6 Parents usually love their children **whichever / whatever** they do.

Exercise 6

Are the highlighted words correct or incorrect in the sentences?

1 **Whatever** ❏ you do, don't leave this cake in the oven too long!

2 It's your party, Amy. You can ask **whichever** ❏ you want.

3 **Whatever** ❏ much I spend on clothes, I never seem to look smart.

4 **However** ❏ hard I try, I can't seem to make any progress.

5 You can fly there or take the train – do **whenever** ❏ suits you better.

6 Get some cheese and olives and **whatever** ❏ else looks tasty.

28

Phrases for talking about time

In this unit you learn to use phrases for talking about actions in the near future.

You can use different time phrases with the verb **be**.

be (just) about to

You use **be (just) about to** to say that you expect something that you planned to happen soon. You can use **just** or not – the meaning is the same. You use **be (just) about to** with the infinitive of the verb.

*Hey, Sara! I **was just about to ring** you.*
*Rob **was about to make** some coffee when the phone rang.*

be on the point of

You use **be on the point of** in a similar way to **be (just) about to**. You use **be on the point of** with **-ing** or a noun.

*By the time they finished the marathon, they **were on the point of collapse**.*
*I **was on the point of going** home when my boss called me into his office.*

be all set to

You use **be all set to** to say that you are ready to do something. You use **all set to** with the infinitive of the verb.

*Are we **all set to go**?*
*Tina **was all set to tell** him what she thought of him, when he apologized for what he'd said.*

be in the process of

You use **be in the process of** to say what you are in the middle of doing. You use **in the process of** with **-ing**.

*We're **in the process of refurbishing** the offices.*
*She **was in the process of applying** for holiday jobs when she was interrupted by her friends calling round.*

be on the verge of

You use **be on the verge of** to say you are very near the point of something. You use **be on the verge of** with **-ing** or a noun.

*She **was on the verge of tears**.*
*The company **was on the verge of going** bankrupt.*

be soon to

You use **be soon to** to say that something is going to happen in the near future. You use **be soon to** with the infinitive of the verb.

The Smith family are soon to leave for their new life in Australia.
Ellie and Paul are soon to be married.

Exercise 1

Which sentences are correct?

1 They were all set to leave for their holiday when they realized the car had been stolen. ❏
2 Pepe was on the point of phone an ambulance when he suddenly felt a lot better. ❏
3 The company had been struggling for a while and was on the verge of collapse. ❏
4 I was just about to lock the door when I remembered Lee was asleep upstairs. ❏
5 Jorgen was in the process to clean the house when he found my lost wedding ring. ❏
6 The shop will soon to close due to a dramatic fall in sales. ❏

Exercise 2

Are the highlighted words correct or incorrect in the sentences?

1 Charis is set **to** ❏ become the next Hollywood superstar.
2 Stig was on the verge **for** ❏ tears when his football team lost the match.
3 I'm just **in** ❏ the process of uploading the images now.
4 Irina was on the point **to** ❏ finishing work for the day when her boss gave her something extra to do.
5 We were all set **for** ❏ go to the restaurant when I realized I hadn't booked a table.
6 Mel was **about** ❏ to switch off the TV when something interesting came on.

Exercise 3

Choose the correct word or words.

1 I was on the point **of / to / for** assuming you weren't coming.
2 Recent improvements meant that the country was on the **verge / process / set** of becoming relatively affluent.
3 Many people become celebrities for a short time, **soon / all set / just about** to be forgotten.
4 Do come in – I'm **just about / on the point / in the process** to put the kettle on.
5 If everyone's ready, I think we're **in the process / on the verge / all set** to go.

Exercise 4

Complete the sentences by writing one word in each gap.

1 Barry's soon _____ retire.
2 Meg's _____ the verge of quitting her job.
3 Gerry's in the _____ of buying a new house.
4 Pip's on the point _____ asking for a pay rise.
5 Fiona's all _____ to become the 100-metre sprint champion.
6 Sheila's just _____ to take off on her first solo flight.

Exercise 5

Choose the correct word.

1 I was on the **process / point** of shouting to my friend across the road when I realized it wasn't her.

2 The performers are all **set / verge** to go on stage.

3 The company is **point / soon** to make dramatic changes to its organizational structure.

4 Ned had been just **about / set** to open the letter when he noticed it wasn't for him.

5 Frederick's in the **point / process** of selling his old computer equipment.

6 Jill had been on the **verge / process** of booking a holiday when her boss said she couldn't have time off work.

Exercise 6

Find the wrong or extra word in each sentence.

1 Fred was just about to go to jogging when he realized he'd left his trainers at the sports centre.

2 Dee was on the point of giving in to when she suddenly became more confident.

3 Sonia was not in the process of painting her room when she ran out of paint.

4 Caroline was on the verge of wishing to him happy birthday when she realized it was the next day.

5 Miguel was about all set to go to music college when he decided to study business instead.

6 Lynda was soon to give of birth to her first child.

Exercise 7

Decide if the pairs of sentences have the same meaning.

1 **A** Dan was about to have a bath when the doorbell rang. ❑
  B The doorbell rang just as Dan was going to have a bath.

2 **A** She was on the point of leaving work when her boss arrived. ❑
  B She had just left work when her boss arrived.

3 **A** I was just about to text you to see if you were coming. ❑
  B I just texted you to see if you were coming.

4 **A** Erika looked as if she was on the point of tears. ❑
  B It looked as if Erika was going to cry.

5 **A** We're about to launch an exciting new product. ❑
  B We will launch an exciting new product very soon.

6 **A** He was on the point of inventing a lie when she interrupted him. ❑
  B She interrupted him because he had lied to her.

29

Using *so* correctly

Inversion after *so* and using *so* to avoid repetition

In this unit you learn how to use **so** in different ways in sentences in order to avoid repeating verb structures.

so + inversion

When you use **so** at the beginning of a clause, you invert (change the order of) the auxiliary verb and the subject. The meaning of **so** in these sentences is **too**. For example:

> *I love chocolate and **so does** Beverly. (= I love chocolate and Beverly loves chocolate too.)*
> *The action film sounds good but **so does** the comedy. (= The action film sounds good and the comedy film sounds good too.)*

so used at the end of a clause

You can use **so** as a pronoun in an answer to a question. When this is the case, you put it at the end of the clause. You use **so** in this way with the stative verbs **hope**, **think**, **suppose**, **be afraid**, **believe**, etc.

> *A Are we in time for the film?*
> *B I **hope so**! (= I hope we are in time for the film.)*
>
> *A Is the cafe upstairs?*
> *B I **think so**. (= I think the cafe is upstairs.)*
>
> *A Can I borrow your car, Dad?*
> *B I **suppose so**. (= I suppose you can borrow my car.)*
>
> *A Have I missed the bus?*
> *B I'm **afraid so**. (= I'm afraid you have missed the bus.)*
>
> *A Is Candy going out with Robert?*
> *B I **believe so**. (= I believe Candy is going out with Robert.)*

do so

You use **do so** to refer to an action that you have already mentioned.

> *If you want to get a drink before the play starts, **do so** now. (= If you want to get a drink before the play starts, get a drink now.)*
> *Anyone who hasn't given me their email address, please **do so** by the end of the lesson.*
> *(= Anyone who hasn't given me their email address, please give me your email address by the end of the lesson.)*

*She tripped up the step and in **doing so**, dropped all the bags she'd been carrying. (= She tripped up the step and in tripping up the step, she dropped all the bags she'd been carrying.)*

You also use **do so** in an answer to a question.

A It's freezing in here! Shall I close the window?
*B Yes, please **do so**. (= Yes, please close the window.)*

A Put those files away before you go home, will you?
*B I've already **done so**. (= I've already put those files away.)*

so after *say* and *tell*

You also use **so** after **say** and **tell** in sentences and as an answer to a question.

A How do you know that Mary is going to be late?
*B She **said so**. (= Mary said that she was going to be late.)*

*I know Andy's coming to see you because he **told me so**! (= I know Andy's coming to see you because he told me he was coming to see you.)*

Exercise 1

Match the two parts.

1 Can I have another cake?

2 Will we see Lorena later?

3 Shall I sit down?

4 I know she loves me.

5 I like watching late-night movies.

6 Have all the tickets gone?

a I hope so. She's great fun.

b I'm afraid so. You're too late.

c Yes, please do so.

d I suppose so. But make it your last.

e She told me so.

f So does she.

Exercise 2

Choose the correct word.

1 **A** Are we in time for the film?
   B I **hope / know** so.

2 **A** How do you know she doesn't like him?
   B She **told / said** me so.

3 **A** Is that Keith's mother with him?
   B I'm **hope / afraid** so.

4 **A** Mel's decided to take that job in Australia.
   B I **believe / think** so.

5 **A** Should I open the window?
   B Please **don't / do** so.

6 **A** Did you say the train was at half past?
   B I **suppose / think** so.

Exercise 3

Which sentences are correct?

1 She skied over the mountain and ended up in another country so. ❑

2 You aren't going out because I said you so! ❑

3 Wayne likes football and so does Coleen. ❑

4 I know she doesn't eat junk food because she told me so. ❑

5 If you would like to help yourself to the buffet, please do it so. ❑

6 They crossed the river and in doing so, entered another state. ❑

Exercise 4

Find the wrong or extra word in each sentence.

1 I like Picasso's work and so does so Carina.

2 If you want to keep complaining then don't go ahead and do so. I'm not listening anymore.

3 She decided to ski off piste and so in doing so crashed into a tree.

4 If I don't know whether Sue's design won the architecture award but I hope so.

5 Mickey likes composing music for on his computer and so do his friends.

6 Johnny attended a casting session for a modelling job and in doing so did won a fantastic contract.

Exercise 5

Put the correct answer in each gap.

B I hope so! I'm desperate for some sun.	**B** I believe so, but I'm afraid we can't afford to buy you one.
B I suppose so, but don't be too late back.	**B** Yes, please do so.	**B** Let me check… yes, I'm afraid so.
B I hope so. Otherwise it's too late.	**B** I think so. Well, that's what they said on the forecast.

1 **A** Shall I put the light on so you can see what you're doing?

_____

2 **A** Meg's parents got her a new computer.

_____

3 **A** Can I go shopping with my friends after school today?

_____

4 **A** The doors are closed! Have we got the wrong day for the concert?

_____

5 **A** Can we afford to go away this year?

_____

6 **A** Is there going to be a full moon tonight?

_____

Exercise 6

For each question, tick the correct answer.

1 Is Maria coming round later?
❑ I know so.
❑ I think so.

2 Do you think I'll get into university?
❑ I hope so.
❑ Please do so.

3 Oh, no! Have I missed the beginning of the film?
❑ I suppose so.
❑ I'm afraid so.

4 How do you know Mario's performing at the Charter Theatre?
❑ He told me so.
❑ He said to me so.

5 Shall I pay the money in when I go to the bank?
❑ Please do so.
❑ I believe so.

Exercise 7

Decide if the pairs of sentences have the same meaning.

1 A We know that they were together last night because they said so.
B We know that they were together last night because they told us that they were. ❑

2 A Ben asked me to take my shoes off at the door and I did so.
B I took my shoes off at the door because Ben asked me to. ❑

3 A If you haven't handed in your homework yet, please do so tomorrow.
B I do not want to wait until tomorrow to receive your homework. ❑

4 A They're getting married in May – they told me so.
B I spoke to them and they said they were getting married in May. ❑

5 A If he wanted to contact me, he'd have done so already.
B He will call me when he wants to contact me. ❑

30

Question tags

have you, did you, will you?

In this unit you learn to use non-basic question tags for checking and emphasizing information.

> To: Linda Jones
> From: Freda Taylor
> Subject: Thanks!
>
> Hi Linda
>
> Thanks for looking after my flat while I was away. I hope nothing happened, **did it?** All my plants look great. You didn't have to water them every day, **did you?**
>
> I'd like to take you out for lunch to say thank you. Let's go to that new Chinese restaurant, **shall we?** You do like Chinese food, **don't you?**
>
> I'm right in thinking you're free on Fridays, **aren't you?** Let me know if this Friday is OK. I'd better book a table, **hadn't I?** It will be busy because it's new.
>
> Love
> Freda

If you have a belief about something and you want to check that it's true, or if you want to find out if someone agrees with you, you can make a statement and add a question tag to make it into a question.

> You haven't been here before, **have you?**

If you are making a negative statement and want to check that it is true, you use a positive question tag.

> You **didn't ask** her about school, **did you?**
> She **should've** had her exam results by now, **shouldn't she?**

Question tags take the same verb as the main verb in the statement they are attached to, as in the examples above. If the statement does not include an auxiliary verb, a modal verb or **be** as a main verb, you use **do**, **does** or **did** in the question tag.

> You think purple's a bad colour for a car, **don't you?**
> She hates me, **doesn't she?**

You can use question tags to show your reaction to what someone has said. For example, you can show interest, surprise, doubt or anger. In this case you use a positive statement and a positive tag.

*Oh, you **think** I'm stupid, **do you**?*

A I've used all the shampoo.
*B Oh, you **have, have you**? I'll have to buy some more now.*

When you use an imperative, you can be more polite by using **will you**, **would you** or **won't you**.

*Be quiet, **will you**? I'm trying to concentrate.*
*Tidy your room now, **would you**?*
*Make me a cup of tea, **won't you**?*

When you use a negative imperative, you only use **will you.**

*Don't tell Chris what I said, **will you**?*

You can also use **will you** and **won't you** to emphasize anger or impatience.

*Hurry up, **will you**? We're already half an hour late.*
*Shut up, **won't you**? I'm sick of hearing your voice.*

You use the question tag **shall we** to make a suggestion using **let's**.

*Let's start again, **shall we**?*

You use the question tag **shall I** after **I'll**.

*I'll let you know if I'm going to Sue's later, **shall I**?*

Exercise 1

Match the two parts.

1 You will come,		**a**	shall we?
2 He never phoned again.		**b**	did he?
3 Don't forget,		**c**	do you?
4 So you think that's amusing,		**d**	will you?
5 I am right,		**e**	aren't I?
6 Let's go,		**f**	won't you?

Exercise 2

Are the highlighted words correct or incorrect in the sentences?

1 You would hardly expect her to know that, **wouldn't you** ☐?
2 Take a seat, **won't you** ☐?
3 We've had much more work lately, **hadn't we** ☐?
4 The new teacher won't know our names, **will she** ☐?
5 Nobody knows that you're leaving, **does he** ☐?
6 Get me a glass of water, **would you** ☐?

Exercise 3

For each sentence, tick the correct question tag.

1 We'd better go,
- ❏ wouldn't we?
- ❏ didn't we?
- ❏ hadn't we?

2 Nothing came in the post,
- ❏ didn't it?
- ❏ did it?
- ❏ did they?

3 I've been doing it properly,
- ❏ didn't I?
- ❏ aren't I?
- ❏ haven't I?

4 The weather's fantastic in Ibiza,
- ❏ isn't it?
- ❏ hasn't it?
- ❏ wasn't it?

5 Nothing will happen to them,
- ❏ will they?
- ❏ won't it?
- ❏ will it?

6 We'd never have known,
- ❏ had we?
- ❏ would we?
- ❏ did we?

Exercise 4

Complete the sentences by writing one word in each gap.

1 Nobody comes here after ten o'clock at night, do _____?

2 You won't forget to post that letter, _____ you?

3 There'd never been problems with that customer before, had _____ ?

4 There should have been a warning sign on that bend, _____ there?

5 Let's ask the waiter to take our photo, _____ we?

6 He can hardly still love her after all that, _____ he?

Exercise 5

Complete the text by writing the correct question tag in each gap.

Max: Hi Eva, sorry. You've been waiting ages for me, [1] _____?

Eve: Hi Max. The thing is, you never arrive on time, [2] _____? Anyway, let's get something to eat, [3] _____? I'm starving!

Max: Well, now, you won't get angry, [4] _____?

Eve: Why? I'm always a very calm sort of person, [5] _____?

Max: Normally yes, but you see, I don't quite know how to tell you this. I guess I'd better just say it, [6] _____? I've left my wallet at home so you'll have to pay.

Eve: You're joking! First I wait ages then you tell me I have to pay for your dinner! Goodbye Max!

Exercise 6

Decide if the pairs of sentences have the same meaning.

1 **A** You didn't go to the party, did you?
   B Did you decide to go to the party? ❑

2 **A** Felix hasn't taken his exam yet, has he?
   B I don't think Felix has taken his exam – do you know? ❑

3 **A** You've never really liked her, have you?
   B Am I right in thinking that you've always disliked her? ❑

4 **A** Paula wants to be a scientist when she's older, doesn't she?
   B Will Paula like science when she's older? ❑

5 **A** You don't believe anything that I'm saying, do you?
   B Do you think I'm telling the truth? ❑

Answer key

1 Compound nouns

Exercise 1

1 b   4 c

2 d   5 e

3 a

Exercise 2

1 aid   4 alarm

2 card   5 mobile

3 travellers' 6 fiction

Exercise 3

1 hairdryer   4 health club

2 side road   5 housewife

3 laptop   6 car wash

Exercise 4

1 science textbooks ✓

2 projects managers ✗

3 drink dispenser ✗

4 arm chair ✗

5 parkingmeter ✗

6 girl bands ✓

Exercise 5

1 ear rings ✗   4 hand bag ✗

2 sunglasses ✓   5 cheque book ✓

3 creditcard ✗   6 memorystick ✗

Exercise 6

1 lady doctors   4 sales assistants

2 women teachers   5 science degrees

3 boy bands   6 Heavy goods vehicles

Exercise 7

1 table tennis   4 knowledge

2 dressmaking   5 careers

3 sleeping   6 washing

Exercise 8

1 Sunbathing   4 steering

2 office   5 tongue

3 season   6 stars

Exercise 9

1 e   4 a

2 c   5 d

3 b

2 Countable and uncountable nouns

Exercise 1

1 the papers   4 room

2 fruits   5 light

3 exercises   6 travels

Exercise 2

1 coffee   5 music

2 chocolates   6 cheeses

3 room   7 exercise

4 noise

Exercise 3

1 Ice forms when water is at or below freezing point.

2 Origami is the craft of folding paper to make models of animals, people and objects.

3 As e-book readers become increasingly popular, they are having a growing impact on bookshops up and down the country.

4 Rents in this town are very high because so many students are looking for accommodation while they are at university.

5 Far greater effort is required if we are to get rid of poverty.

6 A few years ago, cats overtook dogs as the most popular domestic animal in the UK.

Exercise 4

1 Yes   4 Yes

2 No   5 No

3 No   6 No

Exercise 5

1 the guitar   4 ice creams

2 work   5 The noise

3 papers   6 milk

Exercise 6

1 The ✓   4 The ✗

2 the ✗   5 the ✗

3 the ✗   6 the ✓

Exercise 7

1 No   4 No

2 No   5 Yes

3 Yes

Exercise 8

1 d	4 c
2 a	5 f
3 b	6 e

Exercise 9

1 Times
2 the computer
3 research
4 travel
5 businesses
6 work

Exercise 10

1 the violin when she was only 3 years old.
2 the coffee that she usually likes to drink.
3 the panda is still an endangered species.
4 sugar is very fattening.
5 invented the telephone.
6 wood is cheaper than coal at the moment.

3 Adjectives as nouns

Exercise 1

1 e	4 d
2 a	5 c
3 f	6 b

Exercise 2

1 first	4 fourth
2 worst	5 tallest
3 most	6 farthest

Exercise 3

1 Only the best is good enough for my boss.
2 The French have always produced good wine.
3 We were the last to arrive.
4 The biggest isn't always the best value for money.
5 Ted went on holiday the week before last.
6 His second album is great.

Exercise 4

1 unemployed	4 rich
2 good	5 British
3 sick	6 best

Exercise 5

1 No	6 Yes
2 Yes	
3 No	
4 Yes	
5 No	

4 Adjectives + to-infinitive

Exercise 1

1 d	4 c
2 e	5 f
3 a	6 b

Exercise 2

1 far	4 wasn't
2 enough	5 for
3 too	6 weren't

Exercise 3

1 hot	4 healthy
2 wet	5 old
3 good	6 walk

Exercise 4

1 enough	4 far/much
2 to work	5 weren't
3 for us	6 astonished to

Exercise 5

1 David isn't very difficult to persuade.
2 It's not easy to find good restaurants.
3 It's too hot for me to work.
4 The tea isn't hot enough for Max to drink.
5 Pat was amazed to see his friend on TV.
6 The dress was far too small for Sally to wear.

5 Using adjectives in phrases to talk about people and things

Exercise 1

1 d	4 a
2 f	5 c
3 e	6 b

Exercise 2

1 an absolutely	4 absolutely
2 a rather	5 extremely
3 completely	6 quite

Exercise 3

1 believable, important, satisfied
2 possible
3 satisfied
4 legal
5 convenient
6 responsible

Exercise 4

1 mile	3 kind	5 page
2 moving	4 good	6 old

Exercise 5

1 irresponsible
2 two-hour
3 five-degree
4 slow-moving
5 two-minute
6 amoral

---

6 Participle clauses

Exercise 1

1 No
2 Yes
3 Yes
4 Yes
5 No
6 No

Exercise 2

1 Being ✗
2 having ✓
3 being qualified ✓
4 Rejecting ✗
5 Protected ✓
6 not having achieved ✓

Exercise 3

1 Yes
2 No
3 Yes
4 No
5 Yes

Exercise 4

1 Separated
2 Having learnt
3 Learnt
4 Having shared
5 Separating
6 Learning

Exercise 5

1 Having
2 Having practised
3 Having been injured
4 Getting lost

Exercise 6

1 Stopped
2 Having been recognized
3 Not having travelled
4 Taken
5 Not having been
6 Having been allowed

---

7 Expressions to show the purpose of actions and people

Exercise 1

1 b
2 d
3 f
4 a
5 e
6 c

Exercise 2

1 to
2 order
3 as
4 that
5 not
6 so

Exercise 3

1 A party was arranged to celebrate the team's success.
2 Jeremy walked as slowly as he could so that he wouldn't reach home before his parents had gone out.
3 They built a brick wall round their garden in order to prevent rabbits from getting in.
4 The book has been organized thematically so as to highlight developments over a period of time.
5 More research needs to be carried out, in order to confirm the validity of the findings.
6 Many people choose to go to university in order to command a higher starting salary when they enter employment.

Exercise 4

1 so as not to
2 so that
3 in order to
4 in order not to
5 so that

Exercise 5

1 Yes
2 No
3 No
4 Yes
5 Yes
6 No

---

8 Expressions to show the connection between events and situations

Exercise 1

1 Yes
2 No
3 No
4 Yes
5 Yes

Exercise 2

1 whereas ✓
2 As ✓
3 Since ✗
4 while ✗
5 as ✗
6 since ✓

Exercise 3

1 No
2 No
3 Yes
4 No
5 Yes
6 Yes

Exercise 4

1 my brother likes the comfort of a hotel.
2 there's no need to cancel our walk.
3 as one may not be able to come immediately.
4 since she was born in the States.
5 while going by road is slower but you travel door to door.

Exercise 5

1 a
2 c
3 d
4 e
5 b

Exercise 6

1 Since
2 whereas
3 While
4 as
5 while

Exercise 7

1 Yes
2 No
3 No
4 No
5 Yes
6 No

9 Adverbs to show opinion about situations

Exercise 1

1 b
2 f
3 e
4 a
5 c
6 d

Exercise 2

1 to be honest
2 surprisingly
3 Fortunately
4 Apparently
5 Presumably

Exercise 3

1 Yes
2 Yes
3 No
4 Yes
5 No

Exercise 4

1 Understandably
2 Frankly
3 Strangely
4 Unbelievably

Exercise 5

1 fair ✓
2 According to me ✗
3 To our astonishment ✓
4 Wisely ✓
5 with luck ✗
6 for ✗

10 only / hardly / scarcely / quite / very much

Exercise 1

1 b
2 c
3 a
4 e
5 d
6 f

Exercise 2

1 The man only wanted to find out what the old lady was doing.
2 We had scarcely entered the club when we had to leave.
3 I very much regret now that I ever helped him.
4 He was so confused that he hardly knew what to say.
5 I quite enjoy tennis, but I really prefer squash.
6 Losing such a good customer was quite a disaster.

Exercise 3

1 No
2 Yes
3 Yes
4 No
5 Yes
6 No

Exercise 4

1 Yes
2 No
3 Yes
4 No
5 Yes

Exercise 5

1 very much ✓
2 hardly ✗
3 quite ✓
4 only ✗
5 scarcely ✓
6 quite ✓

11 Mixed conditionals

Exercise 1

1 No
2 Yes
3 Yes
4 No
5 No
6 Yes

Exercise 2

1 wouldn't have fallen over
2 has signed
3 hadn't bought
4 knows
5 has taken
6 would hurry up

Exercise 3

1 didn't do ✓
2 lost ✗
3 might have been chopped down ✓
4 you'd give ✓
5 we'd finish ✗
6 could have done ✓

Exercise 4

1 don't tell
2 should
3 went

4 doesn't know

5 wouldn't have been

6 didn't they pay

Exercise 5

1	Yes	4	No
2	No	5	Yes
3	Yes		

12 Expressions for interpreting past actions

Exercise 1

1 might have won

2 can't have finished

3 can't have been

4 must have left

5 could have picked up

6 could have bought

Exercise 2

1 I couldn't have written that in French.

2 Ron must have taken the bus to work.

3 The rain might have caused the accident.

4 She might have decided to go home early.

5 You couldn't have chosen a better course.

6 The postman must have delivered the letter to the wrong apartment.

Exercise 3

1	gone ✓	4	had ✗
2	forget ✗	5	felt ✓
3	have ✓	6	to ✗

Exercise 4

1 must have worked

2 can't have seen

3 could have phoned

4 might have gone

5 mustn't have posted

6 must have got

Exercise 5

1	Yes	4	No
2	No	5	Yes
3	No	6	Yes

Exercise 6

1 The burglar can't have got in through this window because it's too small.

2 Tina's not here, she must have already gone.

3 They must have missed the bus.

4 Do you mean you might have eaten something bad?

5 He might not have listened to your phone message yet.

6 I couldn't have managed without you.

13 Modals in the past

Exercise 1

1	c	4	a
2	f	5	e
3	d	6	b

Exercise 2

1 I should have asked for your help.

2 Should I have come earlier?

3 Frank didn't need to take the bus because he got a lift.

4 Ought we to have put the dishes in the dishwasher?

5 You needn't have tidied up because I was going to do it.

6 I needn't have worn a suit because everyone else had jeans on.

Exercise 3

1 ought to have asked

2 needn't have prepared

3 should have arrived

4 ought to have stayed

5 needn't have spent

6 shouldn't have eaten

Exercise 4

1	Yes	4	Yes
2	No	5	Yes
3	No	6	No

Exercise 5

1 should have told

2 ought to have contacted

3 needn't have made

4 didn't need to have

5 should have sent

6 ought to have explained

14 Modals for expressing feelings about actions

Exercise 1

1	c	4	e
2	a	5	f
3	b	6	d

Exercise 2

1 needs	**4** didn't
2 will	**5** will
3 would	**6** Will

Exercise 3

1 will	**4** didn't
2 would	**5** Dare
3 will lend	**6** tidying

Exercise 4

1 Yes	**4** No
2 Yes	**5** Yes
3 No	**6** No

Exercise 5

1 How often would you go swimming when you were a kid?

2 Will you get the picnic ready while I find the beach towels?

3 I daren't tell you what he said; you'd be furious.

4 Do you think this pasta needs cooking a bit longer?

5 Simon will sing that same song every morning and it drives us all mad!

6 The lawyer said the contract needs translating into Spanish.

Exercise 6

1 Yes	**4** Yes
2 Yes	**5** No
3 No	

15 Verb + object / noun / adjective

Exercise 1

1 c	**4** a
2 f	**5** e
3 b	**6** d

Exercise 2

1 My new socks turned the sheets blue in the wash.

2 The hairdresser dyed my hair bright red!

3 I made the soup too spicy.

4 The council elected me mayor.

5 Janice reported her cat missing.

6 The jury found him guilty.

Exercise 3

1 green	**4** impossible
2 a fool	**5** unhelpful
3 cross	**6** stolen

Exercise 4

1 The students elected Jim president.

2 I painted the room blue.

3 She considers Ross intelligent.

4 They called me boring.

5 He finds the situation funny.

6 She makes me angry.

Exercise 5

1 the baby ✓	**4** alone ✓
2 her ✓	**5** sent ✗
3 to ✗	**6** that ✗

Exercise 6

1 Yes	**4** Yes
2 No	**5** No
3 Yes	**6** No

16 Using whether and that to make statements

Exercise 1

1 whether	**4** Whether
2 whether	**5** if
3 that	**6** that

Exercise 2

1 that	**4** whether
2 If	**5** whether
3 whether	**6** that

Exercise 3

1 No	**4** Yes
2 No	**5** No
3 Yes	**6** Yes

Exercise 4

1 No	**4** Yes
2 Yes	**5** Yes
3 No	

Exercise 5

1 that	**4** if
2 whether	**5** Whether
3 Whether	**6** that

17 Reporting with passives

Exercise 1

1 were expected

2 is believed

3 was found

4 was declared

5 has been referred

6 is expected

Exercise 2

1 The vote has been declared invalid.

2 The man was thought to be Seth's brother.

3 The accountant was found to be stealing clients' money.

4 The manager is expected to be held responsible.

5 The cost is estimated to be $5,000.

6 It was believed that Beatrice would win.

Exercise 3

1 No   3 Yes

2 No   4 Yes

Exercise 4

1 was suggested

2 was declared to be

3 understood to be making

4 was thought to have been built

Exercise 5

1 considered to be ✗

2 was found to have lied ✓

3 was referring to as ✗

4 used to be believed ✓

5 reported as being ✓

6 are expected to be publishing ✗

Exercise 6

1 but it is understood that an announcement will follow in the next two weeks.

2 it is known that drugs can harm the growing baby.

3 are thought to be related to diet.

4 even though it was accepted that it would be difficult to reach agreement.

5 but he is believed to have lived in the sixth century BC.

18 Using adjectives to talk about habits, expectations and obligations

Exercise 1

1 get used to   4 is not supposed

2 Hadn't   5 is bound to

3 had better not

Exercise 2

1 No   4 No

2 No   5 Yes

3 Yes   6 No

Exercise 3

1 Yes   4 Yes

2 No   5 No

3 No

Exercise 4

1 better bring

2 to fail

3 supposed to visit

4 get used to

Exercise 5

1 getting used to   4 are bound to

2 had better not   5 wasn't supposed to

3 aren't supposed to   6 wasn't used to

Exercise 6

1 because I'm used to going to bed late.

2 because she is used to looking after her younger brother and sister.

3 that he wasn't used to eating a big meal at lunchtime.

4 because she was used to her boss including her in all decisions.

5 because I wasn't used to being spoken to in that way.

19 Future in the past

Exercise 1

1 d   4 f

2 e   5 b

3 a   6 c

Exercise 2

1 hadn't   4 had

2 charged   5 bored

3 been   6 got

Exercise 3

1 No   4 Yes

2 Yes   5 Yes

3 No

Exercise 4

1 wished   4 stayed

2 had   5 was

3 kept   6 had

Exercise 5

1 is   4 had

2 had   5 went

3 remembered   6 hadn't

20 Future perfect

Exercise 1

1 married	4 discovered
2 contacting	5 recovered
3 researching	6 going

Exercise 2

1 c	4 b
2 e	5 f
3 a	6 d

Exercise 3

1 Yes	4 Yes
2 No	5 No
3 Yes	6 No

Exercise 4

1 will have lived	4 Ariane will have
2 Will Colin have	5 Tim will not have
3 We will have	6 I will have

Exercise 5

1 has been trying
2 haven't had
3 will have decided
4 has been having
5 will have been marching
6 hasn't left

Exercise 6

1 I have been taking antibiotics because of a chest infection.
2 Fiona will have been living abroad for five years next month.
3 I don't think the plans will have been approved by May.
4 Will the new chief executive have been appointed by then?
5 Both of the children have been behaving brilliantly all morning.
6 Remember that Douglas won't have seen the documents before the meeting.

Exercise 7

1 has been written ✗
2 won't have cooked ✓
3 been meeting ✗
4 will have been waiting ✓
5 won't have been working ✓
6 will have deciding ✗

Exercise 8

1 will have told
2 will have noticed

3 won't have worked
4 will have managed
5 won't have read
6 will have arrived

Exercise 9

1 will have finished
2 have been studying
3 has been
4 will be celebrating
5 have been doing
6 will have had

21 It's time + *past simple / continuous*

Exercise 1

1 No	4 Yes
2 No	5 Yes
3 Yes	

Exercise 2

1 have ✗
2 could speak ✓
3 were setting off ✓
4 is given ✗
5 's had ✗

Exercise 3

1 left	4 wouldn't
2 didn't	5 moved
3 could	

Exercise 4

1 started
2 hadn't made
3 were encouraged
4 were
5 had been decorated
6 didn't make

Exercise 5

1 would call	4 had
2 hadn't told	5 'd had
3 went	6 lived

Exercise 6

1 No	4 Yes
2 No	5 No
3 Yes	

22 Perfect and continuous infinitives

Exercise 1

1 I'm so glad to have met you.
2 We happen to be going to New York soon.
3 I pretended to be waiting for a bus.
4 Did the woman seem to have been crying?
5 I would like to have visited the museum.
6 I'm happy to have been able to help you.

Exercise 2

1	Yes	4	Yes
2	No	5	No
3	Yes	6	No

Exercise 3

1	No	4	Yes
2	Yes	5	Yes
3	No	6	No

Exercise 4

1 He demanded to be told the truth.
2 This book appears to be missing a chapter.
3 Our family is believed to have descended from an ancient Celtic king.
4 This car is guaranteed to have passed the toughest safety checks.
5 The rock band is rumoured to have been seen shopping in our local supermarket.
6 The nurse says my brother seems to be feeling much better today than he was yesterday.

Exercise 5

1	not	4	to
2	have	5	having
3	be	6	been

23 Group nouns

Exercise 1

1	was	4	are
2	is	5	needs
3	get	6	is

Exercise 2

1	is	4	Are
2	isn't	5	were
3	was	6	aren't

Exercise 3

1	is ✓	4	are ✓
2	get ✗	5	is ✗
3	seems ✓	6	need ✗

Exercise 4

1	b	4	e
2	d	5	f
3	c	6	a

Exercise 5

1	were ✓	4	was ✓
2	is ✓	5	are ✗
3	insists ✗	6	were ✓

Exercise 6

1	No	4	No
2	Yes	5	No
3	Yes	6	Yes

24 Phrasal verbs

Exercise 1

1 give them a lift somewhere in a car.
2 cause it to happen.
3 decide that it should not happen.
4 enjoy their company.
5 accept it even though you do not like it.
6 do something nice for someone to try and compensate for upsetting them previously.

Exercise 2

1	out	4	along
2	into	5	up
3	back	6	away

Exercise 3

1	on	4	back
2	up	5	over
3	for	6	off

Exercise 4

1 their relationship
2 a cheque
3 political change
4 such dishonesty
5 her earlier statement
6 a larger company

Exercise 5

1	No	4	No
2	Yes	5	Yes
3	No	6	Yes

Exercise 6

1	brought about	4	stood by
2	hung up	5	broke off
3	got away with	6	caught up

25 Using wh- clauses as nouns

Exercise 1

1 d
2 e
3 a
4 b
5 f
6 c

Exercise 2

1 I'm not sure what to do.
2 We never discovered how it got there.
3 Why she left home is a mystery.
4 Did she admit what she had done?
5 Do you know why he didn't arrive?
6 How she got there is unclear.

Exercise 3

1 where
2 long
3 what
4 when
5 what
6 why

Exercise 4

1 which ✗
2 how ✓
3 Where ✓
4 what ✓
5 how ✗
6 when ✓

Exercise 5

1 e
2 c
3 d
4 b
5 f
6 a

Exercise 6

1 how
2 who
3 which
4 how many
5 how much
6 why

Exercise 7

1 No
2 No
3 Yes
4 No
5 Yes
6 No

26 Relative clauses with prepositions

Exercise 1

1 to
2 in
3 for
4 on
5 from
6 of

Exercise 2

1 e
2 f
3 c
4 a
5 b
6 d

Exercise 3

1 Yes
2 Yes
3 No
4 Yes
5 No
6 No

Exercise 4

1 who
2 with
3 to
4 on
5 that
6 for

Exercise 5

1 Marie is someone who I often confide in.
2 *Greens* is a restaurant that I rarely go to.
3 Eating out is something that we can economize on.
4 That is the project on which I'm currently working.
5 It's a problem which I can relate to.
6 He's a colleague on whom I can depend.

Exercise 6

1 what she was worrying about.
2 which girl he had gone out with.
3 in which my father was brought up.
4 who she had shared a house with when she was a student.
5 what he was writing about.

27 Using wh-ever correctly in sentences

Exercise 1

1 d
2 c
3 f
4 b
5 a
6 e

Exercise 2

1 Whatever
2 whichever
3 However
4 whichever
5 Whatever
6 Whoever

Exercise 3

1 b
2 f
3 a
4 e
5 d
6 c

Exercise 4

1 however you want to.
2 whatever you want.
3 whichever you want.
4 whatever you do!
5 whatever we wanted.

Exercise 5

1 However	4 whichever
2 whatever	5 whenever
3 However	6 whatever

Exercise 6

1 Whatever ✓	4 However ✓
2 whichever ✗	5 whenever ✗
3 Whatever ✗	6 whatever ✓

28 Phrases for talking about time

Exercise 1

1 Yes	4 Yes
2 No	5 No
3 Yes	6 No

Exercise 2

1 to ✓	4 to ✗
2 for ✗	5 for ✗
3 in ✓	6 about ✓

Exercise 3

1 of	4 just about
2 verge	5 all set
3 soon	

Exercise 4

1 to	4 of
2 on	5 set
3 process	6 about

Exercise 5

1 point	4 about
2 set	5 process
3 soon	6 verge

Exercise 6

1 Fred was just about to go jogging when he realized he'd left his trainers at the sports centre.

2 Dee was on the point of giving in when she suddenly became more confident.

3 Sonia was in the process of painting her room when she ran out of paint.

4 Caroline was on the verge of wishing him happy birthday when she realized it was the next day.

5 Miguel was all set to go to music college when he decided to study business instead.

6 Lynda was soon to give birth to her first child.

Exercise 7

1 Yes	4 Yes
2 No	5 Yes
3 No	6 No

29 Using so correctly

Exercise 1

1 d	4 e
2 a	5 f
3 c	6 b

Exercise 2

1 hope	4 believe
2 told	5 do
3 afraid	6 think

Exercise 3

1 No	4 Yes
2 No	5 No
3 Yes	6 Yes

Exercise 4

1 I like Picasso's work and so does Carina.

2 If you want to keep complaining then go ahead and do so. I'm not listening anymore.

3 She decided to ski off piste and in doing so crashed into a tree.

4 I don't know whether Sue's design won the architecture award but I hope so.

5 Mickey likes composing music on his computer and so do his friends.

6 Johnny attended a casting session for a modelling job and in doing so won a fantastic contract.

Exercise 5

1 **B** Yes, please do so.

2 **B** I believe so, but I'm afraid we can't afford to buy you one.

3 **B** I suppose so, but don't be too late back.

4 **B** Let me check... yes, I'm afraid so.

5 **B** I hope so! I'm desperate for some sun.

6 **B** I think so. Well, that's what they said on the forecast.

Exercise 6

1 I think so.	4 He told me so.
2 I hope so.	5 Please do so.
3 I'm afraid so.	

Exercise 7

1 Yes	4 Yes
2 Yes	5 No
3 No	

30 Question tags

Exercise 1

1 f	3 d	5 e
2 b	4 c	6 a

Exercise 2

1 wouldn't you ✗   4 will she ✓

2 won't you ✓   5 does he ✗

3 hadn't we ✗   6 would you ✓

Exercise 3

1 hadn't we?   4 isn't it?

2 did it?   5 will it?

3 haven't I?   6 would we?

Exercise 4

1 they   4 shouldn't

2 will   5 shall

3 there   6 can

Exercise 5

1 haven't you   4 will you

2 do you   5 aren't I

3 shall we   6 hadn't I

Exercise 6

1 No   4 No

2 Yes   5 No

3 Yes

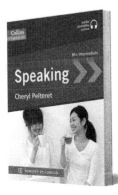

Collins

Work on your Grammar
Over 200 exercises to improve your English grammar

A1 Elementary
978-0-00-749953-3

B2 Upper Intermediate
978-0-00-749963-2

A2 Pre-intermediate
978-0-00-749955-7

C1 Advanced
978-0-00-749967-0

B1 Intermediate
978-0-00-749962-5

Work on your Vocabulary
Hundreds of words to learn and remember

A1 Elementary
978-0-00-749954-0

B2 Upper Intermediate
978-0-00-749965-6

A2 Pre-intermediate
978-0-00-749957-1

C1 Advanced
978-0-00-749968-7

B1 Intermediate
978-0-00-749964-9

collins.co.uk/elt

 collinselt

POWERED BY COBUILD